Praise for *Home in Exile*

Home in Exile reads like a novel telling a story that transcends generations and continents. It is a story of identity and ideology, of courage and cowardice, of patience and power. It is the story of the best of faith seeking to deny the worst of religion. It is the story of one family's attempt to keep their country on its path of pluralism and peace. *Home in Exile*, however, is not a novel but a true story told by a daughter-granddaughter-wife-mother who wanted to serve her grandparents' country by serving others. You will not be able to put it down as you reflect on what its keen insight offers you, wherever you may be."

—**Chris Seiple**
Former President of the Institute for Global Engagement and the founder of the Council on Faith & International Affairs

"Set against the backdrop of India's shifting socio-political landscape, *Home in Exile* is more than a memoir—it is a call to remember, to resist, and to heal. It is a courageous and deeply moving testament to faith, family, and resilience in the face of political, spiritual, and personal upheaval. Through evocative prose, the author leads us into the heart of a family legacy rooted in service, love, and intergenerational strength—only to reveal how that very legacy is tested by betrayal, bigotry, and the forces of rising nationalism.

The tamarind trees that frame the narrative are a powerful metaphor: ancient, rooted, bearing witness to joy, injustice, and endurance. What struck me most was the Liz's unwavering honesty and her ability to hold grief and grace in the same breath. Her voice is prophetic yet grounded, tender yet unflinching. This story will resonate deeply with anyone who has ever struggled to belong, to speak out, or to reconcile love for a homeland with sorrow for what it has become.

—Lalita Iyer
Indian author and journalist

IN EXILE

*Where She Uncovered the Freedom
to Write Her Own Story*

LIZ MATNEY

MEDIA.COM

Home in Exile
Copyright © 2025 by Liz Matney

All rights reserved. No part of this book may be reproduced in any form or by any means—whether electronic, digital, mechanical, or otherwise—without permission in writing from the publisher, except by a reviewer, who may quote brief passages in a review.

The views and opinions expressed in this book are those of the author and do not necessarily reflect the official policy or position of Illumify Media Global.

Published by
Illumify Media Global
www.IllumifyMedia.com
"Let's bring your book to life!"

Paperback ISBN: 978-1-964251-74-5

Cover design by Debbie Lewis

Printed in the United States of America

Contents

Acknowledgments vii
Introduction ix
Prologue xiii

1   The Silent Witnesses 1
2   A Heritage Rooted in Faith 7
3   A Rising Storm 21
4   An Unnecessary Battlefield 30
5   My Return to India 38
6   In Search of a Place to Heal 49
7   Hanging on to the Good 57
8   The Shadow of Fascism 65
9   A Christmas Message of Hope? 72
10 Finding Stillness in Sant Cugat 79
11 US Citizens Unlawfully Detained 87
12 Vigilant and on Edge 94
13 Abrupt Transitions 101
14 Freedom Unfolding 106
15 Reflections In Flight 113
16 The Stillness That Speaks 120
17 When Mountains Move 125
18 The Legacy That Moves On 132

Acknowledgments

This book was not written in a vacuum. It was written in the thin air between exile and home, between heartbreak and hope, between what was lost and what must never be forgotten.

First, I thank God, not some source of empire or exclusion but the God of light who sat with me in the darkness. The one who did not flinch at my anger, who heard my questions, who stayed.

To my husband, parents, siblings, and children, thank you for loving me when I was lovable and when I was not. For holding the thread when I was unraveling. For praying when I couldn't find the words. For being my home when the world felt hostile.

To Philip and Janet, thank you for seeing a writer in the rubble. For saying, "You can do this," when I could only whisper, "I don't know how."

Joannie, you helped me write my very first book proposal at a time when the police were stealing laptops and vandalizing my parents' home. (Yes, the Damoh police returned it. Even they must have sensed the sacred in a stolen story.) Thank you for praying, for persisting, and for introducing me to Michael, who listened to the cracked, trembling voice inside me and said, "There's strength here. There's a story here. Let's tell it."

Karen Bouchard and Geoff Stone, you are weavers of broken threads. Thank you for sitting with the mess, for not being afraid of my jagged sentences or tangled trauma. You helped me make sense of it all—without sanding off the edges.

Chris Seiple, thank you for believing in me when I felt invisible, like a ghost in my own story. You reminded me I still had a voice.

Lalita Iyer, thank you for showing me the dignity of rawness, the beauty of baring one's soul without shame. Your generous endorsement was more than words; it was solidarity.

To Jen and the copyediting team: thank you for the quiet, unseen labor of polishing the prose without erasing the pulse. You helped this book walk upright.

And to those who sent their blessings and prayers,— I'll always remain grateful!

Introduction

This is a story about faith, betrayal, and ultimately redemption. It takes place mostly in India and is the story of the impact of a country in turmoil on a family with generational wounds. Some names have been modified. However, those familiar with the events will likely recognize the real people behind the narrative. This is not an exposé but rather an honest reflection of experiences that continue to shape me.

I write about the *imili* trees around my grandparent's home. These trees serve not only as a memory of a special place but also as a metaphor for the complex realities I try to make sense of: the tension between holding on and letting go, the weight of inheritance, and the strength sometimes found in deep roots. While writing about resilience, belonging, nostalgia, and the layered nature of personal and collective histories, the presence of these trees grounds this work, both literally and symbolically.

There are those in these pages who may be cast in an unflattering light- some might even say as villains. I won't pretend to understand the choices they made or the harm that resulted. The truth is, I still struggle to reconcile how people capable of love and goodness can also be capable of causing so much pain, especially to those they call their own.

And yet, weather heroes or villains, I want them to know I still love them. In my own way I am still working toward peace with it all.

You know, many of the dynamics of this story remind me of what happens when a woman is assaulted. Women are often told to let it go. Keep your composure. Smile. Forgive. Move forward. Especially if the perpetrator is someone close to the family, or God forbid, part of the family, then vulnerability is bound up like nobody's business. Don't name names. Don't call them out. Don't rock the boat.

I've been advised to do the same thing with this story.

But I can't do that.

In this book, I'm calling out the bullies.

I'm not a victim. I am a victor because God's promises are strong, and prayers are still powerful.

I can only acknowledge what occurred from my standpoint. There are many complexities of the mess that I may never understand. But my standpoint matters. It gives me a voice to express what I have seen and experienced from my unique vantagepoint. And when I don't allow that voice to be silenced, it can inspire a shift in the status quo maintained by bullies in positions of power. This is the beginning of healing.

And if you have experienced oppression or persecution in your life, I want you to know that the same truth applies to you: Your standpoint matters. Your voice matters.

This book is dedicated to all who are silently crying out, desperate to break the silence. Now is the time to

Introduction

heal. Healing broken spaces begins with acknowledging what is broken.

May all that is lost be restored according to God's will. Amen.

Prologue

Our cars had been stopped in the middle of Marutal village. The air was filled with familiar smells of the earth, wood, and smoke, the darkness punctuated by the eerie glow of torches and the murmurs of a growing crowd. Special forces had been sent to our home by the state. And for what? To illegally detain my family when all we had ever done was serve those around us. The police officers swarmed without a warrant. Hours of agony and confusion!

Some reporters hovered like vultures with cameras ready to capture our disgrace, while the police—two hundred strong now—milled about like a pack of wolves waiting for the signal to strike. Yet among them were those who stood tall, their pens, cameras, and duties wielded not as weapons but as instruments of truth.

Those journalists, the officers, the people of Damoh bore witness to our rawness with integrity that honored it. Their questions were thoughtful, their presence a quiet testament to the belief that even in our most fragile moments, there was dignity worth preserving.

The resilience of our people surrounded us with strength and prayers to combat the night's heavy darkness. But not all came in service of truth. Some who hovered, were there to frame our suffering as a headline designed to sell. Whatever they captured—whether with grace or greed—was released to the world. The news went viral. Our vulnerability, our plight, was laid bare for all to see.

And yet, as those images spread like wildfire, thousands dropped to their knees in places far and near, hands clasped in prayer for people they may never meet. Strangers wept for us. They felt the hollow ache of losing a place called home, of being stripped from the land that cradled the bones of our ancestors. They understood, in some quiet place within themselves, the pain of belonging torn away.

Inside the car, these prayers helped me stay calm so as not to frighten my twelve-year-old son, any more than he already was. My husband was sitting in the front seat.

He turned around and asked our son, "You doing okay, buddy?"

Our son, trying to keep humor alive, said, "Daddy, if they try to open my door, I'm ready to pull a Mike Tyson one-two on them."

We were exhausted and our perseverance was being tested. I rolled my window down, desperate for a crack of reason in the madness. A female officer passed by, her uniform stiff, her expression harder. I caught her eye.

"There's a kid in this car," I said, forcing assertiveness in my voice. "You're probably a mother, right? You know children shouldn't be a part of all this."

My words, meant to stir her humanity, were met by coldness. She smirked. She spit out her words like they were cheap, mocking me with the sarcastic use of the word *friend*:

"Oye, yaar. Kitna bolti hai."

I wasn't her *yaar*.

"Watch your tone when you talk to me," I said, each syllable sharp as broken glass.

Suddenly, a shout pierced the night.

It was the voice of my mother pleading with an officer who stood, chest puffed and his ugly moustache twitching like some absurd caricature of authority.

"Your husband is the accused criminal!" the man bellowed, his ugly beer belly shaking as though his cruelty had given him power.

1

The Silent Witnesses

In the beginning, before the fractures—before the deep divides that would cleave the land I once called home—there was a house.

This was not just any house but the house of my *dada* and *dadi*—my grandfather and grandmother. The once-grand abode stood, stubborn and ancient, like an organism grown from the very earth itself. The house had sheltered generations and stood witness to the ebb and flow of a family steeped in history.

The foundation of this house was far more than brick and mortar—it was stories and silences, laughter and tears. The house absorbed everything—every echo, every breath. The creak of the floorboards whispered secrets, while the windows groaned with the weight of everything that had come before. It was more than a family home. It was a sanctuary, a testament to who we were, where we had come from, and what we strived to become.

As a child, when I innocently wandered those halls, I never could have imagined that the feeling of belonging that the house so effortlessly carried could ever be questioned.

This was the house where Donald McGavran, a famous missionary to India, had been born, and his legacy lingered quietly in every corner. It was a constant reminder of the path my grandparents chose—a life of devotion to God, service to others, and sacrifice.

The very stones and beams of that house represented the weight of generations committed to a higher purpose, and in time I came to understand that. But as a child, to me it was simply home. A place where sunlight streamed through tall, stately windows, casting long shadows across dusty floors. A place where the faint scent of incense that filled the air mingled with the sweet tang of tamarind trees outside the windows.

Ah, the tamarind trees—the towering *imili*—loomed over the garden like ancient sentinels. Their twisted roots dug deep into the earth, much like our family's roots in this land. The trees were not just silent witnesses to our childhood games; they held the essence of our past, whispering to us from beneath their broad, leafy canopies. My cousins and I gathered tamarind in overflowing sacks that spilled into every storeroom, every corner of the house. The sticky sweet-sour pulp clung to our fingers, lingering on our tongues long after we had pulled apart the pods. We climbed those trees, laughing so hard we lost all sense of time. It felt like the world beyond could never touch us.

But something was stirring. Perhaps, the safety of those branches might not last forever.

The garden, like the house, was a world of its own. It stretched far and wide, with rows of flowers and vegetables that my dada tended with a devotion I admired but did not yet understand. He loved nature, his plants, his pets, just as deeply as he cared for people. On cool mornings, I would sit with him and his ever-faithful Doberman, fondly named Prince. Sipping chai as steam curled into the crisp air, I listened to my grandfather's stories of Europe and America, lands where my parents, grandparents, and great-grandparents had studied.

"The first time I traveled to America," Dada told me more than once, "it was a six-month journey by sea. I would write letters home to your Dadi."

I would close my eyes and imagine my grandmother's joy as she received each letter from the love of her life, marked with the stamps from a far-off land. Even though I could feel that warm, loving feeling rising, the whole narrative was as strange for me as it is for my children to imagine that there once was a time when our lives operated without access to the internet.

There was so much I soaked in with naivety. After all their studies and travels, all the great-grandparents and grandparents shared a history of always returning back to India. I never cared to ask why. Did their sense of duty really run as deep as the roots of the tamarind trees? I loved hearing all those stories but was too young to ask questions like: What was life like for you in the new post-independent India? In college, what was your experience in America as a non-white person? Did you ever encounter any storms in the midst of all your international travels by sea? There was too much innocence for any of those questions to even phase me at that time.

It was in that garden, on one of those mornings that I first heard the word *Hindutva*—though I wouldn't fully grasp its meaning until much later. Some people dressed in white kurtas had come to have tea in the garden. Dada's face, usually so calm, had a subtle shift in expression, but it was not an outright rejection of the term. It was as though he recognized the shifting tide—one that had both the potential for pride in cultural identity and the risk of something far more divisive.

I didn't ask then, but I wish I had. Perhaps that was when I should have realized that something in the world beyond our home was shifting. But how could I have known that the India I knew and loved was slowly changing? That it was not only the garden, the tamarind trees, or our home that would be tested, but the very idea of who belonged here?

Though I was born in North Carolina, my identity was deeply tied to this land, to this house. To me, India was a vibrant mosaic of festivals, friends, and family. We celebrated everything—Diwali, Holi, Christmas, Eid—with equal fervor.

The divisions that existed in the world outside blurred within our walls—or so it seemed. After all, we were all Indian, bound together by shared history, shared joy, and the rhythm of life in this country. But joy, like all things, is fragile. And peace, once disturbed, is difficult to restore.

Holi was always a burst of color, Diwali loud and joyous as the sky blazed with firecrackers. And Christmas—oh, Christmas!—was the highlight of the year. The birth of the Messiah, our Savior! Our home would fill with hundreds of people from every walk of life, from every faith, gathered for the grand Christmas tea party. Everyone was welcome: Hindus, Muslims, Sikhs, Christians, and those claiming no faith in particular. It was more than tradition; it was the embodiment of the unity that had always defined us, the unity that defined India. But in time, that sense of oneness would be tested in ways we could never have imagined.

It was during a Raksha Bandhan celebration that I first sensed a shift in the wind. The night before, my cousins and I made rangoli patterns on the floor using colored rice, sand, and flower petals. Our hands stained with henna, and our giggles filling the air. The next morning, my sisters and I tied colorful *rakhis* bracelets on our brothers' wrists, and they joked about how it was "rip-off-your-brothers day." Our rakhis did not cost much, but the brothers showered us with presents. We embraced any excuse to bring the family together and to celebrate.

But amidst our laughter, I noticed something—a tension I couldn't place. Though I didn't realize it at the time, there was a brief moment when my dada's smile faltered, and he glanced over his shoulder, as if sensing something I was too young to understand.

I heard the adults whispering again, this time more urgently. Something the kids couldn't fully comprehend had taken on a darker meaning. No longer was it just some distant political discourse; there was a storm brewing, growing into something closer, more threatening. There were some tensions that the children couldn't fully sense, let alone comprehend. On the outside there were anti-conversion laws in Madhya Pradesh, the second-largest state in India. There were glaring signs of a strange new reality. Meant to prevent forced conversions from Hinduism to another religion, these laws were now weaponized, used against those who dared practice their faith openly. For my family, these weren't just laws. They were instruments, misused to vilify our monotheistic worldview. These laws were often instruments misused to act as direct threats, attacks on our way of life and sense of home.

For generations, my family had served India with love, spreading Christ's message with open hearts, not force. Historically, Christians in India have touched the untouchables, cared for the outcast, and embraced the abandoned. But now, we were being vilified, painted as enemies in our own land. Suddenly, home didn't feel like home anymore.

As children, we didn't understand the changes in the political landscape. All we knew is that a shadow had descended on our beautiful lives, and our home didn't feel like home anymore. There were talks of sending the kids off to boarding school.

The tamarind trees still stood tall. Their leaves swaying gently in the breeze, but the world beneath them had changed. The house, once a sanctuary, now felt like a relic of a fading time. Festivals continued, but now they were marked by an undercurrent of fear. An unspoken question lingered: What if this was the last Raksha Bandhan we celebrated together?

2

A Heritage Rooted in Faith

My childhood home still stands like a sentinel of the past. Its walls are thick with the stories of those who had walked through its corridors long before I was born. It is a place where identity and belonging are woven into every stone, every breath of air. But even in a house like that where the collective identity is so interwoven, it is sometimes hard to know where you truly belong as an individual. It is hard to reconsider one's sense of home when generations before you have bled and built and believed in a vision- a God-given vision of family, of community. To leave a place like that, to be pushed out of it, is to question everything you thought you knew about who you are. Perhaps it's a blessing in disguise.

Dada Vj spent decades building a community, one rooted in faith and service, something he inherited from those before him. But the impact of the Christian faith on our lives—and the lives of those around us—didn't begin with my grandfather. It actually began with his grandmother—my-great-great-grandmother—a woman whose act of faith and courage has echoed through every generation since.

My great-great-grandmother, born into a wealthy Hindu family, defied the caste expectations of her time. In a world where conversions were seen as a betrayal—something reserved for those who were desperate to leave the caste system or for those aligned with the British colonialists—she found something far deeper in the pages of the New Testament. Teaching at a missionary school, she learned about Jesus, and in those teachings, she found a love that transcended societal boundaries.

But love comes with a price. When her in-laws discovered her newfound faith, they plotted to end her life, viewing her conversion as a disgrace. Her maid recognized the plotting from the shadows and warned her of the danger. In the dead of night, clutching her two-month-old baby boy, she fled. She sought refuge with the missionary women she had worked alongside. Those women took her in and named her son Samuel Law. Her own life was claimed soon after—some say it was the plague; some say it was murder. Only God knows the truth.

Samuel, my great-grandfather, grew up under the care of those missionaries, and in time, he sailed to the United States for his higher education. The thought of traveling by ship for six months—a journey today's generation couldn't imagine—was a testament to his perseverance. He went by himself on that passenger ship, no GPS or mobile phones, just the vast, unending ocean and the vision of something greater on the other side. He was not just crossing seas; he was building bridges between worlds. Samuel returned back to India after finishing his higher education.

When India gained its independence in 1947, Samuel's British and American missionary family left the country. They returned home, but India was his home. He stayed behind, alone once more, and became the principal of the mission school where he grew up. It was here that he met a young English teacher named Martha, whose quiet strength mirrored his own. They fell in love and had three children: Vj, Stan, and Romona.

Samuel continued his work, laying the foundation for education in the region. His vision was not just about classrooms; it was about community. It was about building a place where all people—Hindus, Christians, Muslims, and those claiming no faith—could find common ground, could be cared for, could belong, could flourish.

Samuel's oldest son, Vj—my grandfather—inherited that vision. As a boy, he studied at prestigious English schools in big cities, but when he was fifteen and studying hours away, his mother fell gravely ill. Untreatable, they said. It was some mystery illness that left no time for goodbyes. Stan, his younger brother, was left behind to shoulder the domestic responsibilities caring for their six-year-old sister while the weight of family expectations pressed down on his young shoulders.

That moment defined both brothers in ways that would haunt the family for decades to come. On the outside, all seemed well, but the paths they would walk from that point were drastically different, and the growing chasm between them would set the stage for generational tensions to come.

Vj carried his grief like a mantle and channeled it into service. Like his father, Vi made a commitment to serve his motherland. After studying at Butler University in the United States, he returned to Damoh, Madhya Pradesh, with a vision that stretched far beyond the confines of his own personal loss. He started the first school for the blind and the first English-medium school (a school where English is the primary language of instruction) in Damoh. He became the president of the rotary club, carried out several humanitarian initiatives, and brought people together from every corner of society. He enjoyed the company of those who maintained drastically different worldviews and found common ground through their appreciation for creative, intellectual, and social pursuits. Everyone from Indian mystic Osho to Mother Teresa visited my grandparent's home. Vj and his wife, Pusha, saw no divisions in caste or religion—only a common humanity, something that had been etched into his very soul by his father. The hospitals they helped establish weren't just buildings with beds and doctors; they were sanctuaries for the broken and the needy, places where people could come to heal, not just physically but emotionally and spiritually.

Vj's younger brother, Stan, on the other hand, carried his grief like a stone in his chest, one that grew heavier with every year. He saw every opportunity slip through his fingers. While Vj was out shaking hands and casting a vision of unity, Stan often felt simmered in the background. Outwardly, he seemed to find joy as a teacher at the local school, but inwardly he bore the weight of the admiration that his older brother commanded so effortlessly. Perhaps he believed that he deserved better

A Heritage Rooted in Faith

for all those years of serving his home and family during the time of his mother's death. Vj carried a sense of both guilt and responsibility toward his brother. This resulted in Vj putting his brother on a public pedestal whenever he found an opportunity. But regardless of the honor and recognition, Stan's unhealed wounds trickled down into future generations like a thread that unraveled too slowly for anyone to notice until it had woven itself into the lives of those who came after, twisting itself like a vine that no one knew how to prune.

In the quiet moments, when the air was still and the sun had begun to crawl across the sky, there was an unspoken truth: one always sought the warmth of the other but could never hold it for long enough to feel its full embrace. One would lift the other, placing him on a pedestal that gleamed too brightly to touch, a high place where the weight of expectation rested like a heavy cloak.

It wasn't that love was absent. No, it was there in all its tangled, complicated beauty. But it was often a love that did not heal—did not mend the things that needed mending. And in the end, the wound remained, carried forward in ways that would affect the lives that followed, the generations who had no choice but to live with it, though they never quite understood how it had arrived. Sometimes we don't even realize that we are carrying the weight of something that came long before us.

In time, the world would change, as it always does. But the echoes of that love, that complex, fractured love, would linger. It would speak through the silence. It would make its mark on the future, carving paths that could not easily be erased. And those who came after would learn to walk within it, just as they had learned to breathe.

Vj's two sons, Dave and Aj, grew up watching their parents serve selflessly. In time, another bloodline—the Fenry's—became woven into the fabric of this great family saga. My nana and nani (maternal grandfather and grandmother) Dr. Doug Fenry and his wife, Usha, were longtime friends of Dada and Dadi (Vj and Pusha). Doug was a quiet, humble man, but his accomplishments spoke volumes. One of the first Indian plastic surgeons trained in England, he was mentored by the renowned missionary Dr. Paul Brand, who had revolutionized treatment for leprosy patients. Dr. Doug had devoted over four decades of his life to the leprosy mission in rural Central India, and together with Usha they had built a life of service, grounded in faith.

Usha herself was a remarkable woman. Her father was a Bengali Brahmin who had converted to Christianity, an act of defiance in its own right, while her mother was an Israeli Jew. The Fenrys' marriage was a union of faiths, cultures, and legacies, and together they embodied the essence of what it meant to serve Christ in a world divided by caste, religion, and politics.

As their family grew, so did their bond with Vj and Pusha's family. It seemed almost providential when Vj's two sons fell in love with Doug and Usha's two daughters, Sheja and Inu. Their love stories were simple, but their unions were significant. It wasn't just two couples coming together—it was two legacies intertwining, two families rooted in service and love becoming one. Both families maintained a firm legacy of leadership, always guided by the example of Christ and His perfect love, the kind that is beautifully described in 1 Corinthians 13.

Dave married Sheja, and Aj married Inu. Together, they carried forward the legacy their parents had built, expanding the reach of their family's work in both India and abroad. Vj's sons had found love and partnership with women who shared their legacy, vision, and faith. Dave built his work with his father, while Aj and Inu wanted to carry the legacy forward carving out their own unique path. While choosing their different paths, the two brothers focused on keeping respect and unity alive within the family and the community.

But with this blessing of building for their community, this joy of giving, came greater jealousy. Initially, it came not from strangers but from faces we had known since childhood, voices that once called our names with affection became curled with envy, masked in politeness but sharpened by hidden agendas.

We were told, as children are in families with long roots and longer memories, that the people of Damoh are our people. Ours in the way riverbanks belong to the river. Ours in the way ancient trees remember who planted them. But what does it mean to belong to one another? There were those cousins—in heart, if not by blood—who sought to drain the legacy dry, to dip their hands into a lineage they neither tended nor understood. They mistook the family's name for a throne, and the memories it carried for a weapon.

Legacy without surrender becomes possession. It wasn't long before cracks in the foundation began to show. And so we stood grateful but wary, learning to carry our inheritance lightly—not to be owned but to be held with trust. Outside the walls of the home, the political landscape of India was shifting, moving toward an aggressive nationalism that sought to divide communities along societal and religious lines. This shift in India would further divide and undermine everything my grandparents, great-grandparents, and even great-great-grandmother had sought to build.

Those who aligned themselves with the small-minded goons who were part of the rising nationalistic movement used the political climate to their advantage. Emboldened by their local political connections and longstanding resentment, they began to plot against their very own. Damoh began to feel like a different place for our family.

For Dave and Aj, family relationships meant a sacred trust, something to be guarded and nurtured, passed down with integrity and humility. But darkness that had crept into the cracks, just as it had into the nation, and it would not be easily dispelled. The political tide in India turned toward something more sinister. It was the age-old battle between light and darkness. While the country pretended to be the world's largest democracy, it functioned as a fascist regime in disguise. Power, greed, and jealousy masqueraded as brotherhood, and the very relationships that should have been a source of strength became the battleground for something far more destructive.

A Heritage Rooted in Faith

For Dave and Aj, the challenge wasn't just the rise of religion-based nationalism or the political unrest that threatened each of their individual paths. It was the betrayal that came from the people they thought were their very own. It was the realization that sometimes the greatest threats aren't from the outside world. They're from the people you trust the most.

As this story unfolds, what becomes clear is that the battle between light and darkness is never just a metaphor. It is real, and it is personal. It is a story as old as time, and as relevant as ever. What Vj and his sons fought to preserve wasn't just a legacy of faith but a vision of home, of belonging, of what it means to truly serve others. And that vision was under siege.

How could I forget that imili tree! My grandfather often sat under its shade during his final days when he was enduring his last stages of cancer. Those trees provided a place of comfort under which Dada finished writing his last books, and before he passed on to the life beyond, he left the land on which the imili trees grew to his dear sons.

The trees stood on the land like steadfast witnesses, their roots curling deep into the earth, entangled with the stories of generations. They were as old as the soil itself. Gnarled and wise, their branches were heavy with the sour tamarind that we children used to pluck in the afternoons, laughing as we chewed the puckering fruit, our faces twisting in delight. The imili trees were more than just plants around Dada and Dadi's home and garden; they were unflinching observers, still watchmen to countless monsoons and summers, to laughter and tears. Those trees heard the murmurs of secrets carried on the wind, soaked in the sun of better days and the shadows of the darker ones.

Vj's children and grandchildren often stood by those trees long after he had passed. We rested our hands on the old, rough bark as we gazed over this land—the land my grandparents once walked on, the land where love stories began, where children were raised in the promise of something greater. It wasn't just any land; it was home, the pulse of a legacy that ran deeper than blood, more sacred than any other possession.

But there were those who saw the imili trees differently. Not witnesses to history, not guardians of memories but inconveniences standing in the way of their plans. Land was power. Power was everything. These trees had no place in the new world.

One day, under the guise of neighborly concern and friendly chats, they approached Dave, eyes gleaming with something far darker than affection.

"The land, Bhaiya," that voice low and syrupy sweet. "It's getting crowded. We need more space. And that tree... well, it's taking up so much of it."

Dave, ever the peacemaker, ever the one to offer the benefit of the doubt, looked and nodded, though the words sounded like a screeching sound in his ears. He trusted too easily. Perhaps that was his fault. Or perhaps he was wise enough to know that they weren't really asking; they never truly asked. It was a statement dressed as a favor, a demand draped in silk. If Dave agreed, he'd lose more ground—again. If he said no, his refusal would be twisted into something ugly, something that could cripple like poison. Knowing this, Dave had no option but to give a stiff nod. These ties should never turn into shackles!

Where Dave and Aj saw the family's legacy as something to protect, there were those who saw it as something to conquer. The family's land—rich with history and memories—was nothing more than an asset the greedy hoped to conquer. They had no interest in preserving it; their focus was on leveraging it for personal gain. It wasn't just about building a house or cutting down trees. It was about systematically dismantling what had been built, piece by piece. This is what happens when history becomes legend and with time legend becomes myth. The imili tree was the first to fall. To those who cut it down, the tree was just a symbol of an outdated past standing in the way of the future they envisioned. They were trying to rewrite history, but history has roots deeper than memory and echoes louder than myths.

They tried to twist the narrative. They wanted to rename the heroes. They even tried erasing the records. But the truth lingers—stubborn and unyielding—in the soil, in the silence, in the stories passed on from one trembling voice to another. This is what really happens when history becomes legend. Facts may fade but meaning endures. And meaning has a way of finding its way home.

For those who wanted to chop down more trees, their greed was quiet but relentless. They didn't need to raise their voices or make grand gestures. Their actions, subtle and deliberate, spoke louder than any words. They moved with a quiet determination, dismantling the family's legacy with each decision they made, each tree they cut down, each piece of land they claimed. They believed they were building something better, something stronger, but in truth, they were building walls. Those who build walls in the name of religion betray the very essence of faith.

Those same people who had their lives spared during COVID at the Christian Mission Hospital, those same people forgot to offer their support when the petty goons plotted to shut down the mission hospital. Religion at its truest is meant to be a bridge between the divine and the broken, the stranger and the beloved, the sinner and the saint. When religion becomes a fortress to protect power or exclude the "other," it ceases to be holy. When extremists shouted hateful speeches against upstanding people, such hate only mirrored the very fear, pride, and cruelty that they thought they were fighting to heal. Or perhaps these so-called Hindu extremists were just fighting for the sake of their own displaced anger, misusing the name of religion. The God I know, never asked for stones to be cast—only open hands, outreached arms, and a table with more chairs. But in the fog of confusion, we can easily mistake the safety of walls for the presence of God.

In Damoh, the entanglements and co-dependency seemed to run deep. From the moment she got married, my mother, Inu, wanted to make sure she protected herself and my dad, Aj, from the slow poison that she saw growing around the imli trees. She encouraged Daddy to start his own separate humanitarian initiatives, to build his own home, independent of what his father and brother had built, so he wouldn't be dependent on them. God blessed their work, and it grew both nationally and internationally. But with greater success, came more haughty eyes, envy, and greed from their own people.

For the power-hungry, greed creeps in like a whisper, curling around the roots of old friendships, choking them from the inside until only a husk remains. The land—my grandfather's land—was what they coveted most. To them, it wasn't about what it meant or what stories it held. It was about ownership. About staking a claim, about the sheer joy of taking. And so, under that veil of darkness, they hacked away at the imili tree. The sound of the blows reverberated in the still air, each swing of the axe sending splinters of bark flying, as if the tree itself was crying out in protest. It groaned and creaked under the onslaught, its old limbs trembling until, with a final crack, it fell.

When Dave found the stump the next morning, his heart sank. The imili tree was gone. Just like that. A piece of history, of his father's history, severed at its roots. In its place was a scar in the earth, and the rising skeleton of what would be the land they encroached. For them, it wasn't enough to live under the shadow of the leadership that had built it all. They wanted to own it, to twist it to their own ends. And if that meant tearing down what our forefathers had built, cutting away the roots of our very family tree, then so be it.

The imili tree was only the first to fall. There would be others—other trees, other legacies, other lives that they were after. All in the name of power. Dave stood at the edge, staring at the empty space where the tree had once stood. The sour tang of tamarind still lingered in the air, though the tree was gone. He wondered how something so sweet could leave such a bitter aftertaste. The land that was their sanctuary should always be a safe haven, never a point of contention.

As the sun set over Damoh, the imili tree lay in pieces on the ground, its branches scattered like forgotten memories while those that caused riots in the streets thought they stood triumphant, their eyes gleaming with victory. But victory, like greed, is fleeting. And in the quiet, in the stillness of that evening, Dave could almost hear the tree whisper its final secrets to the wind. The land remembers, it said. God is watching, and the land always remembers.

3

A Rising Storm

Across India, in the pale of dawn, groups of men gather to stand in formation, wearing crisp, white shirts and khaki shorts. Their drills and exercises mimic those of a militant organization as they chant "Hindu Rashtra," their voices rising in disciplined unison. Not a whisper. Not a question. A declaration.

These are the members of the Hindu nationalist organization Rashtriya Swayamsevak Sangh (RSS), and they believe they are safeguarding something sacred and protecting what they love most about India. Their India.

RSS was established in 1925. Promoting *Hindutva*— roughly translated as "Hinduness"—RSS members see themselves as the guardians of Hindu culture. They embrace a vision of India steeped in traditional Indian culture without the influence of foreign values or religions. People like me don't fit their fable. Too Indian for the West, too Christian for the new India. I don't care to be a part of a world where history becomes legend and legend becomes myth. But let's first grapple with the natural and the practical. Once that makes sense, then I can then reflect on the supernatural forces that remain at play.

These men gather much like a family protecting its home from an encroaching storm. It's an impulse we all recognize, an idea that isn't foreign to Americans—or to anyone, really. It resonates in the hearts of any people who understand the weight of identity and nation, who feel the stakes that come with protecting what we think defines us.

In India, this yearning finds its embodiment in Hindutva, a movement that asks a fundamental question: Who gets to claim the soul of the nation? Hindutva seeks to offer clarity in a chaotic world where identity feels fractured. Its message is one of restoration—a return to something purer, simpler, and more unified. A vision of India that existed, or so it is said, before it was tainted by foreign influences.

And who can blame us for defending what we cherish? Isn't that part of the human condition? A struggle for belonging, yes, but also a deeper struggle for recognition, for the right to be seen and known as who we are, even if that effort leaves us shattered, misunderstood, or even dangerous.

Because sometimes that kind of fervor can lead to embracing darker impulses.

We didn't see it all at once. The storm came in disguises: a law here, a comment there. At first, people called it nationalism or pride. Then, safety. Then, inevitability.

The men who chant in the fields are not monsters. They go home to their mothers, to their wives, to the smell of hot dal and roti. They post selfies on Facebook. They cry when their children fall ill. But they have been taught that love for a country requires the hatred of those who don't look, pray, talk, or marry like them. They have been trained to mistake obedience for righteousness. Trained to see loyalty only in the reflection of their own faces.

And then the rest of us, well, we try to hold onto the India we knew. We clutch it like a fading photograph. An India where we celebrated Holi and Christmas in the same breath in Dada and Dadi's home. An India where we could all sit under the imili tree, and Dada could freely quote the Bible to a man who wore a tilak on his forehead and called him *bhai*.

Inside the house, the walls still hum with old stories. The floor remembers our little feet that danced during Eid, Rakhi, and Easter. But the air is heavier now. The windows don't open as easily anymore.

With the promise of Hindutva comes an undeniable tension. Hindutva claims to restore a pure and unified vision of India, but instead it pushes others to the margins, turning a vision of unity into one of exclusion. Muslims, Christians, dissenting Hindus all become "the other," the unseen, the ignored, the existential threat. In the process, efforts to protect what we cherish can sometimes blur the line between love and fear.

And still some say, "Why are you afraid? Nothing has changed."

But everything has changed. The silences are different now. They come with teeth.

"We are just protecting what is ours," explained an old acquaintance, now loyal to the saffron cause.

I asked him, "What is yours?" He didn't answer. Just looked past me, into a distance only he could see.

Maybe it was grief. Maybe it was power. Maybe, like most things now, it was both. When I looked into his eyes, I saw something different, something unspoken. His eyes were lost, almost like a child who couldn't make sense of a world that no longer resembled what he thought it was. I couldn't help but wonder: was this truly conviction, or was it a fragile shield against a deeper confusion?

This isn't a new narrative. Across the world and across centuries, movements have sought to define who belongs and who doesn't. In America, too, this question of national identity—of protecting a way of life—feels all too familiar. We hear echoes of it in the debates over immigration, race, and culture. Who belongs? Who deserves protection? And what happens when the answers to these questions push others to the fringes?

Inside the walls of a home, stories are easier to share. They are close and breathing; they sleep in the next room, call out for chai, and sit under the shade of the same trees. They argue about small things that are really not small at all. They are stitched into the fabric of everyday life, and so we can talk about something warm and familiar. But outside the walls and the familiar gardens, there are other forces. Cold, nameless, sometimes faceless forces. They hum in the wires overhead, creep in through the cracks beneath doors, curl into the lungs of those we love. They are harder to name and harder still to write about: power, poverty, and history. They move often quietly, sometimes violently between people, chanting what they envision, what they dream of and hope for.

A Rising Storm

As the cold forces rearrange lives, they blur the lines between power and strength—confusing fear for respect, silence for resilience. The shifting of influences and warping of priorities is subtle. What was once precious becomes a burden. What was once unthinkable, or rather unbearable, becomes ordinary. And through it all, the stories inside the home start bending to fit the shape of the world outside. That is where the foreboding seems to unravel.

They say storms can be tracked before they arrive. But this one—this rising storm or ideology and inheritance—was centuries in the making. We should've known. We should've built our shelters when the skies were still blue. But maybe we believed too much in the sun.

Storms can develop suddenly, but generally they come after some warning signs. The sky darkens. Winds feel turbulent. Temperatures drop. Animals become agitated. Beasts in the forests seek shelter.

Meteorologists use the latest technology to track storms, so they can warn individuals to prepare and take necessary precautions. The key is to prepare before the storm.

I have a friend who lived in Oklahoma City, the heart of Tornado Alley. She said that when her parents built their home, they built an underground tornado shelter to protect themselves during severe weather events. "The key is to prepare when everything is calm," she told me. Nobody builds shelters in the middle of the tornado.

The threat to India's democratic principles came in as a rising storm. Yes, there were subtle changes in ideological currents and social tensions that might have helped us prepare, but many of these were overlooked, perhaps because people simply could not fathom the devastation the storm was about to unleash.

The first signs of the storm appeared in 1909. India had been under British influence since the mid-1800s. The struggle for independence was also an identity crisis that divided people groups that had never known what it was like to be one nation.

In a way, isn't that the tragedy we all face? When a nation, like a person, grapples with an identity crisis, we cling to what feels certain. But often, that certainty is fragile, born not out of understanding but out of fear. When we don't know who we are, when the world around us shifts too quickly, we reach for something to hold onto, something to protect us. But what if in our quest to protect ourselves, we become blind to the very people we're meant to care for? What if the real struggle is not just about defending identity but about finding a way to live with our differences?

This is the heart of Hindutva's struggle. While rooted in a desire to belong, it manifests in actions that speak of something far darker: enforcing conformity, silencing dissent, marginalizing those who dare to question its vision of India.

In India, this is the world Hindutva has created for millions—a world where some voices are privileged, while others are drowned out by the deafening noise of mob justice. The privileged are the ones who stand with the majority, but those who drift from that ideology are sidelined.

The battle isn't just in parliament or on WhatsApp or on the streets of Delhi. It's in the language used at the dinner table, in the abridged textbooks, and in the silence of those who once spoke freely. It's in the moment a child chooses not to say their Christian name or Muslim name. It's in the knowing glances exchanged when someone says "conversion" like it's a curse.

And maybe that is the point of storms—not to destroy but to reveal what was already fragile.

Thankfully, the judiciary remains a beacon of hope for balance. But where corruption breeds, imbalance follows. The powerful speak loudly, while the marginalized fade into the background, their quiet cries for recognition barely audible.

And yet, this isn't just about Hindutva, is it? It's about every nation, every society where identity becomes a weapon wielded to exclude rather than include. Could it be that in our efforts to define who belongs we've forgotten that belonging itself isn't something to guard—it's something to share?

When our own inner world is in turmoil, when our cries are silenced, we fall into survival mode. Fight. Flight. Freeze. That's all we know. But how often do we pause and ask ourselves: What are we fighting for? What are we fleeing from? What if instead of protecting issues, we started protecting people?

The fight for identity, for nationalism, for purity—it's all a distraction, isn't it? It keeps us blind to the real, bleeding hearts behind the politics and the rhetoric. It's not India versus the West or Hindus versus Muslims. It's human versus human. It's all of us trying to survive in a broken world.

This chapter of India is not just political. It is spiritual. Existential. It is about whether a country built on pluralism can survive the plague of purity. It is about whether memory can withstand mythology. Whether love can outlive loyalty to flags.

So we return to the land. To the tamarind trees. To the soil that remembers more than we do. And in this gathering storm we ask ourselves: Will we remain rooted?

We speak often about freedom of speech, but what about the freedom to be safe? To live without fear of hate speech, misinformation, or harassment that erodes one's dignity? Should freedom come at the expense of another's humanity?

What if we dared to uphold a higher standard? One where freedom isn't just about saying what we want but about ensuring that others can live in peace? What if instead of shouting over one another, we chose to listen? To speak in ways that reflect not our own need to be heard but the humanity of the person standing opposite us?

These are the questions that linger. The wind is rising. And maybe that's where the grace of God shines brightest—not in the defense of our own rights but in our commitment to the care of others. Not in protecting borders but in ensuring that the people—each made in God's image—within those borders can live with dignity and peace.

A Rising Storm

Some imli trees are still standing—for now. But storms, as we know, have a way of finding even the oldest roots.

In the end, maybe it's not about what we're protecting. Maybe it's about what we're willing to let go of so that others can thrive.

The world is shifting. The cries of the forgotten are growing louder. What happens when they are no longer ignored? If we don't listen soon, the very thing we're trying to protect—our nation, our people, our soul—will slip through our fingers. In our efforts to hold onto identity, we risk losing the very essence of what makes us human.

So, as we stand on this battlefield, the choice is ours. Will we choose compassion or conquest? Understanding or division?

The battlefield awaits.

4

An Unnecessary Battlefield

Long before the British set foot on her shores, India was a land of many faces, many tongues, many gods. There was a sacred chaos held together by mountains, rivers, philosophies, and trade routes. Many have said that rather than homogenizing the land European colonialism often fostered division, emphasizing subcultural, regional, and linguistic differences to maintain control. But colonialism didn't create caste or religious tension; it amplified what already existed. Yet any attempt to unify a nation through political scaffolding doesn't erase old wounds. It simply binds them into a structure. And in time, those wounds began to reopen.

In 1909, the British parliament introduced the Indian Councils Act which opened up Indian participation in legislative councils. With it came a controversial provision: separate electorates for Muslims. For some Hindus, this move was seen as the British legitimizing divisions. For some Muslims, it was seen as a safeguard, a political voice in a system where they feared being outnumbered. The air only grew thicker with tension.

An Unnecessary Battlefield

By then, the Muslim League had already formed, seeking to preserve the cultural and political rights of Indian Muslims. In response, Hindus formed the Hindu Mahasabha to preserve their own heritage and interests. From there, a quiet arms race of ideology began—one not of bullets but of identity.

Into this growing tension stepped Vinayak Damodar Savarkar—a brilliant, radical mind who would shape the ideological foundation for modern Hindu nationalism. Unlike the fluid, often contradictory spiritual traditions of Hinduism, Savarkar offered not a religion but a political and cultural identity: Hindutva. Prior to this cultural shift, Hindus claimed no set creed or dogma. According to Savarkar, however, to be truly Indian, one had to see India as both fatherland and holy land. This, by design, excluded Muslims and Christians.

As Gandhi called for nonviolent unity, a quieter movement—one that saw the pluralism Gandhi cherished as a threat—was taking shape in the background. A young doctor named Keshav Baliram Hedgewar, inspired by Savarkar, founded the Rashtriya Swayamsevak Sangh (RSS) in 1925. The RSS wasn't a political party; it was a cultural project. Discipline, order, and national pride were its pillars. But so too was suspicion—of the West, of minorities, of any worldview that didn't fit their mold.

After Hedgewar passed in 1940, the RSS leadership fell to Madhav Sadashiv Golwalkar, who brought a more aggressive ideological edge. Drawing on fascist theories of ethnic unity, Golwalkar's infamous book *We or Our Nationhood Defined* praised Nazi Germany for its "race pride" and called for a similarly unified Hindu identity. He viewed minorities not as citizens to include but as threats to contain.

When Gandhi spoke of *swaraj*—self-rule rooted in moral authority—Golwalkar envisioned a *rashtra*—a nation purified of foreign influence. When Nathuram Godse, a former RSS member assassinated Gandhi in 1948, the government banned the RSS temporarily, though the organization would later be cleared of direct involvement. Godse's detailed explanation given in the courtroom as to why he assassinated Gandhi was later published and widely circulated as people wanted to know the ideological and political motivations for the murder.

After independence, Nehru attempted to hold India together through secularism—not the absence of religion but its neutrality in state affairs. In a land with so many gods and stories, the constitution offered one unifying narrative: that all were equal under the law. That one could be Muslim, Christian, Atheist, Dalit, or Brahmin and still be Indian.

But not everyone believed in that kind of equality.

As India matured, so too did the political arm of Hindutva. The Bharitiya Jana Sangh, founded in 1951, gave RSS its first foothold in electoral politics. Its ideologies were sharpened under Deen Dayal Upadhyaya who wrote *Rashtra Jeevan ki Disha*. He rejected Western liberalism in favor of a vision rooted in what he interpreted as ancient Hindu values. He spoke of "Bharatiya culture," one that emphasized duty over rights, social order over individual expression. Muslims, he believed, were historical invaders.

An Unnecessary Battlefield

Christians, agents of conversion. Pluralism, according to his worldview, was a Trojan horse.

Though Upadhyaya never called for violence, his ideas laid the groundwork for a movement that would grow more aggressive over time.

After Upadhyaya's death in 1971, Indira Gandhi, Nehru's daughter, rose to power within the Congress Party. Indira Gandhi's authoritarian turn—marked by the Emergency, a twenty-one-month state of emergency declared in the mid-seventies—shook the nation's faith in the Congress party. When democracy returned, the Jana Sangh joined a broader coalition and by 1977 evolved into the Bharatiya Janata Party (BJP).

The BJP's rise was slow at first, but steady. Over time, its message sharpened and Hindutva became not just a cultural philosophy but a political weapon.

Later, when Rajiv Gandhi's Italian-born, Catholic widow, Sonia Gandhi, assumed leadership of the Congress Party, the BJP and its allies intensified their campaign, casting Sonia's faith as a threat to India's Hindu majority and claiming Christian missionaries would seek to convert Hindus under her protection. The BJP's rise spurred the mobilization of Hindu nationalist groups across the country, transforming the political landscape and amplifying a charged and combative political identity.

The storm against minorities gained force, beginning with the brutal violence in Gujarat's Dangs district and culminating in the horrific 1999 murder of Australian missionary Graham Staines and his two young sons, who were burned alive in Orissa.

In 2009, Orissa's Kandhamal district saw another wave of violence. More than six thousand homes were reduced to ashes, and fifty thousand people were displaced. Thousands were injured, and nearly a hundred men and women were savagely killed.

The world watched as Hindutva, fueled by resentments once directed at the British, began to recast its ire on India's minorities—a dangerous alchemy that sowed division rather than unity. Anti-conversion laws multiplied, as did hate-filled public speeches and violent acts. Things that would once cause a national outrage slowly became background noise.

By 2014, the BJP had secured a full majority. Narendra Modi, a former RSS *pracharak* (a volunteer and propagator), became the prime minister. His victory was hailed as a triumph but beneath the promises of progress, an old ideology stirred.

Anti-conversion laws spread. Mob lynchings became more common. Freedom of the press began to shrink. And those who spoke up faced the cost.

In 2017, Gauri Lankesh, an outspoken critic of religion-based nationalism, was shot outside her home in Bengaluru. Her voice had echoed too loudly, they said. Her murder was not just an attack on a person; it was a warning. Government officials who publicly made inflammatory statements about religious minorities faced little to no repercussion.

Prime Minister Modi spoke about India's democracy on international platforms but never commented on such ongoing atrocities in the home he was called to lead. Sometimes silence speaks volumes.

As voices like Gauri's disappeared, others went underground. Civil society was hollowed out. Terms like *secular* became slurs. The word *Christian* was increasingly coupled with *convertor* and *Muslim* with *infiltrator*. During the lead-up to the 2024 elections, Modi openly referred to Muslims using that very word. What began as ideology became structure. And what was once structure could become law.

Prominent Hindutva ideologues like K. N. Govindacharya speak openly about rewriting the constitution to reflect "true Indian values" or their interpretation of Hindu values. Even as some of these ideologues decry colonialism, they ironically cite Cuba's communist constitution as a model: collective interest over individual freedom. The aim is not diversity but dominion.

And yet amidst all this, we remember: India is not one voice. We remember the beautiful anthem on the public television broadcaster Doordarshan in the eighties and nineties, "*Milay sur mera tumahara, toh sur banae humara*" ("When your melody joins mine, a shared tune is born"). The tune is one that speaks not just of individuals but of us together. From the hills to the coasts, there are different rhythms, different languages. From the temples to the mosques, from the elders to the children, when our hearts beat together our homeland sings. The power is not in one voice but strength comes in the co-existence of our differences.

This is still the strength of my motherland. For every hate speech, there is a hand that reaches out. For every tree that is felled in silence, there are roots that remain underground—waiting for the rain.

When my family was dragged through injustice, it wasn't only fellow Christians who stood by us. Some of our strongest allies were devout Hindus—lawyers, neighbors, friends who believed in the spirit of the constitution. People who had nothing to gain and everything to lose. People who chose conviction over convenience.

That is the India I remember when I think of my dada and dadi's home. That is the India my grandparents believed in. That's the India we still hope for.

Hindutva claims to protect something sacred, but it has been misused to desecrate the very soil it claims to love. Its anger, though rooted in legitimate wounds of colonization and cultural loss, has turned into suspicion of anyone who walks a different path. And suspicion left unchecked becomes violence.

There is an old truth: "hurt people hurt people." But healing is also generational.

If there is to be peace, it will not come from uniformity. It will come from remembering that India was always many things at once. That her strength has never been in a single story but in the way stories clash and overlap and endure.

This movement born from the wounds of colonial exploitation and scarred by the emergency declarations of Indira Gandhi has left many leaders bound to a rhetoric of hurt rather than a mission of healing. Fear of deviating from Hindutva's rigid narrative stifles innovation and creativity, breeding a nation where people worry about becoming pariahs if they question the prevailing ideology. After his reelection in 2019, Prime Minister Modi, instead of addressing the devastating farmer suicides, rising mob violence, or record-high unemployment, opted to deride secularism itself, claiming, "not a single political party dared to campaign under the banner of being secular." The guardians of India's secular constitution are left to wonder: has religious nationalism upheld religion as a path to the divine, or has it reduced it to a tool of political identity?

When our family endured hardship, those who stood with us looked at humanity and saw beyond labels of religion, society or politics, reaching instead for the common thread of compassion that binds us all. They knew that the imili tree may fall. But the land remembers. They saw that the land, too, is waiting for justice.

5

My Return to India

By 2022, life had settled into a kind of gentle rhythm. God had given me more than I dared ask for: my devoted husband, Lee, spirited children, and a Colorado home tucked into the stillness of alpine beauty. Our days passed in a rhythmic routine of drop off and pick up at school; dinner tables filled with laughter; beautiful blankets of snow; and the quiet, ordinary rituals of belonging. I loved the simple grace of being a mother, of hosting meals and gathering people around shared stories, warm food, and flickering candles. That act of hospitality felt sacred, an inheritance passed down to me from my grandparents and parents, who loved deeply and well, who welcomed the world with open arms and steady hearts. I had no desire to return to India even though my parents had spent five decades building a sanctuary for our family, a place where we could always return, a place we could all feel at home.

I had no desire to return to India partly because I was content with my life in America, away from the polluted air and the crazy crowds. There was a peace in our small mountain town, a peace that made the chaos of India feel far away. I hadn't longed to return. Not really. Not with the rising tides of nationalism I sensed from a distance, or the quiet foreboding I couldn't yet name. My grandparents had passed on, and with them, the India I had known as a child—the home of towering tamarind trees and long afternoons spent in stories and play—had faded into something more fragile, more uncertain.

India, to me, had become a place of memory, a sanctuary built by my parents with five decades of love and sacrifice I wasn't ready to reclaim. Not yet. The air felt too thick, the crowds too wild, and the responsibility too heavy. And yet... sometimes, life whispers in ways we cannot ignore.

Before the pandemic, the world seemed small, and we could travel wherever we wished. But after lockdowns, there was not only a new realization of the frailty of life but also of the distances that geographical divides can cause. My Midwestern-raised husband had a strong sense that we should go back and spend time in India.

How was this possible that my husband, raised in the heartland of America, felt the call most clearly? "Let's go," he said with a conviction I didn't fully understand. Our Indian friends would often joke that he'd become more Indian than I was, and they weren't wrong. After nearly two decades of marriage, he carried the culture with a kind of reverence I had slowly let slip.

Our children, who were born in India, saw my parents' home in Damoh as paradise. "Papa and Meemaw's place will always feel like home," they'd say, even as they returned to the luxuries of the West. I understood. I had once felt that same way about my dada and dadi and nana and nani's homes. Those were sacred spaces where love lived in every corner, and belonging required no explanation.

So we went. After the long shadow of the pandemic, we returned to India for a month. And to my surprise, something shifted.

I arrived limping—still healing from a brutal car accident—but by the end of our stay, I was running up hills again. My body healed alongside my heart. There was a guesthouse behind my parents' home, a quiet place of rest where we stayed. The children played with their cousins in joy that felt untouched by time. My husband and I laughed again, really laughed, without watching the clock or worrying about childcare. My sister and brother-in-law took the kids for movie nights while we rekindled a sense of wonder.

It felt like grace. Unlooked-for, but unmistakable.

Maa greeted us with feasts at every meal—fresh produce from our farms, the kind of nourishment that doesn't just fill the belly but restores the soul. She paid attention to every detail as though every gesture carried the weight of blessing. I hadn't seen my husband have so much fun with the kids in years. We all felt at home.

Something inside me loosened. I realized how tightly I'd been gripping life in America, clutching it to my chest as if it were the only place we could find meaning. But here, surrounded by family, prayer, and open sky, I felt free again. Free to love, to rest, to let go.

And then, Dadi—my ninety-five year old grandmother—prayed over us, a quiet, profound blessing that I will carry with me always. There are some moments too sacred for words. Her eyes, though tired, still gleamed with mischief and grace. She had always carried herself with a kind of elegant spunk, the kind that made you believe you were witnessing timeless beauty.

But I could see her physical body was fading. Slowly, gently. Yet her presence remained warm, strong, and powerful, there were moments when it seemed like she was already experiencing glimpses of her eternal destiny. In those moments, she was at complete peace, looking up to the heavens with a huge smile on her face.

A month after we returned to Colorado, her time on earth grew short. My sister sent me a video just hours before Dadi passed. In it, she was reaching her arms upward from her bed, eyes full of awe.

"Mama, are you seeing something?" my mother asked.

"Yes, yes," Dadi smiled.

"Are you seeing Papa?" Daddy asked softly.

"Yes," she whispered with a smile.

Dada used to joke that he'd find her in heaven so they could be "stuck together forever." Dadi would shake her head, laugh, and reply, "Vj, one lifetime is quite enough." But in her final hours, there he was, waiting to welcome her into her eternal home.

I sobbed when Daddy called to say she was gone, not just for the loss but because I wasn't there. The house felt suddenly too quiet. The veil between worlds had lifted. Dadi's departure was a bittersweet reminder that the veil is very thin between the temporal and the eternal, between the dimensions that we see and the invisible that surrounds us and goes far beyond our physical beings.

Later that year, my husband and I returned to India, not just to visit but to stay for a while. As we made that decision, we had no way of knowing the extent of growing political antagonism even though many pundits were pointing to it. We didn't foresee the abrupt transitions that would change our family's sense of home forever.

Shortly after we returned to India, it became painfully clear that the charged political climate had reshaped the political and social landscape. Behaviors and attitudes once deemed unquestionably objectionable were now justified by a large portion of the population. The once-peaceful Hinduism of the ancient sages had been overshadowed not by outsiders or enemies but by small-minded men with loud voices and smaller hearts, men who wore religion like armor and wielded it like a weapon.

They didn't chant for peace. They shouted for purity. They didn't fold their hands in reverence. They clenched their fists in suspicion.

The family that once gathered at festivals and around firelight and tamarind trees and shared prayers now found itself watched. Whispered about. Uninvited. Misunderstood because of the local journalists who were out to defame, not because we had changed but because the place around us had started to forget the meaning of its own heart. I did not care to return back to that place that was gradually becoming cruel and merciless.

But I left my peaceful abode and I witnessed them closely. Petty men with shriveled hearts, standing on

My Return to India

brittle stages, spewing hatred into vulnerable crowds. How does one explain to one's children that the place they revered, the land of their forefathers, is the very place where their sense of belonging, our family's name, our faith, our roots—everything—is suddenly reduced to a question mark?

When we arrived in India in the summer of 2022, everything felt hopeful at first. We helped where we could and poured our energy into the work, believing we were planting seeds that would last. And then came August 15, 2022, Svatantrata Diwas, India's independence day. This was just a few weeks after we had returned back to India. The head of state, the chief minister, recognized my father for his exceptional service during the pandemic. Our family had helped install the only working oxygen plant in the district, saving countless lives. It should have been a moment of pride.

Instead, he became a target.

Extremist groups launched a campaign of hatred. They burned effigies of my father. They shouted on local broadcasts: "How could such honor be given to a Christian?" They spread venomous and unchecked lies. Local authorities did nothing. The silence was deafening. People were hesitant to speak against them. Why were they not held accountable? Why are they allowed to roam free, loud, and venomous?

A quiet vendetta was set in motion against my father. Many who sympathized said, "Your greatest crime is that you are Christians." The demonic was parading in the daylight, and they were calling it divine. I saw it happen with my own eyes. As real as the dust that settles on the windowsills in abandoned homes.

God was with us in that darkness. He was silent sometimes but always at work and never absent. The presence of that divine mercy made us stronger. What was meant to harm us only brought us closer to each other. We didn't just survive it; we were shaped by it, sharpened by it because we were able to witness God's miracles in moments when we felt weak. Yes, we have seen miracles in the midst of ruin!

I watched the darkness rise in daylight. Men with shriveled hearts, standing on fragile stages, spewing fear into vulnerable crowds. It was like watching a bad dream unfold with your eyes wide open. My children were scared. Our family was targeted. My father was being hunted—not with bullets but with rumors and intimidation, with targeted inquiries and police threats.

What could we do? We prayed. As a family and as a community, prayers became our lifeline. I gathered weekly with three dear sisters, our hearts breaking open before God. In one powerful hour of prayer something shifted in me. I felt strength return. I thought we were protected. But almost immediately after, all hell seemed to break loose.

That night, I walked into my parents' home and found chaos.

"There's a FIR against Daddy," Maa said, packing his suitcase with steady hands. "There's pressure from high up to arrest him." That is what they are saying, "He's not safe here."

My Return to India

An FIR is a First Information Report and marks the official beginning of a police investigation. I could barely speak. Just hours before, I'd felt shielded by divine presence. Now we were being hunted.

The superintendent of police admitted he was "under pressure." The law was being twisted. Innocence no longer mattered. It was all performance now, spectacle dressed in righteousness.

Even my children sensed it. "Mama, is it true that mobs could come into our campus?" my son asked, referring to the gated area of our home.

"No, Baba," I replied. "Most people are our friends. Nothing bad will happen."

"Can I sleep next to you tonight?"

"Yes," I said, holding him close. "Always."

There is no script for when your twelve-year-old child asks you if he's safe. There is only presence. Only prayer. Only love.

We couldn't use our phones. We had to disappear and hide like fugitives. Like criminals. All for love.

I asked aloud one night, "Why is this happening to us?"

Maa looked at me, and in a calm and clear voice said, "Because we stand for something they don't understand."

I will never forget that.

Some storms cannot be stopped, only survived. We clung to each other. And in the midst of the terror, there were still moments of grace. Like the call from Uncle Raul in the midst of the chaos. He gifted us a beautiful trip to Bandhavgarh. "The jungle awaits," he said. For two days, we watched tigers move through tall grass like living flame. Five sightings. Five sacred moments. Their beauty was feral, unafraid. It was a reminder that survival is its own kind of prayer.

Another unexpected blessing arrived when Lee and I managed to steal a long weekend away to Sri Lanka, a fleeting interlude for just us and our children. Our daughter had a long weekend break from boarding school, and Sri Lanka was just a short flight from Coimbatore. It was a brief escape, yet it felt like slipping into a different world. The air was thick with the tang of salt, and the rhythmic pulse of the waves sang a soothing lullaby. Standing at the edge of the ocean, the cool water lapping at our feet like a gentle whisper, we surrendered our thoughts to the sea, allowing its vastness to wash over us, if only for a moment. In that precious time, we felt the weight of the world slip away. It was replaced by the tender embrace of the ocean's caress, as the horizon stretched endlessly before us, promising both solace and mystery.

We laughed as if the years had melted away, a release that flowed as naturally as the tide. As we watched the sunset transform the sky into a canvas of colors too beautiful to name, I clutched that memory close, knowing it would become a piece of armor against the storm we would soon face again.

"We should bring the whole family next time," Lee said, smiling, his eyes filled with hope. I nodded, imagining the laughter that would fill the air as our whole family played in the waves.

My Return to India

The next day, we ventured into the waves. Seeing we were in one of Asia's premier surfing destinations, we signed up for surfing lessons with the kids. As we paddled out, I felt the exhilaration of the surf beneath us, each wave a challenge that called for balance and strength. Surfing, I discovered, is a dance of perseverance; it builds the core—both physically and metaphorically— and is a reminder of our own resilience. Each attempt to ride the waves became a lesson in determination, a reflection of the struggles we faced together as a family.

But even with these moments of peace, the return to reality always felt heavier, like the weight had grown while we were away.

Still, home no longer felt like home. Every return to Damoh felt heavier, as if the land itself were saying, Your time here is ending.

But we gave everything. We loved without reservation. We planted. We prayed. And when the ground rejected our offering, we stepped back—not in defeat but in reverence.

Some places you love with your whole heart. And then you let go. Not because you no longer care but because the land must choose its own healing.

India does not belong to any one party, any one religion. It belongs to its people. But a nation wounded by fear will always be suspicious of love. It will reject what it cannot control. It will exile its prophets and curse its healers. And yet we remain grateful. Grateful for what was built. For the lives touched. For the love given freely. That, too, is a kind of miracle.

Now, we turn toward healing.

For my parents, who are senior citizens, this season has brought a reimagining of what home means. Not a place. Not even a country. But a belonging that transcends geography.

And for me? I carry the stories. The prayers. The memory of tamarind trees and tigers, of surfboards and supper tables, of laughter through tears. I carry them like seeds. Not to bury, but to plant elsewhere.

Because the light shines in the darkness.

And the darkness has not overcome it.

We are healing and we are grateful. Grateful for each other, for the endurance we found through the kindness, empathy, love, and prayers of people from all walks of life and every corner of the world. Grace held us steady through that nightmare.

6

In Search of a Place to Heal

After centuries of peaceful coexistence in India, our family was suddenly subjected to social and cultural marginalization that stripped us of the chance for emotional and physical well-being. We were called criminals because we are Christians. We had to hide like fugitives. We were not able to use our phones or laptops. We couldn't communicate with our dear loved ones and were left wondering about their safety.

I couldn't help but wonder if those that acted out of malice and those who acted out of political pressures had any capacity for empathy. Their eyes were cold and insensitive, like stone.

Maybe they did not bear the capacity to realize the level of assault they were instigating. If this was their definition of loving their nation, it was a demented perception of love. Love does not subject people to hazards that can cause trauma, sickness, and death, at least never intentionally!

We lifted our pleas to the heavenly throne of God. In moments when we felt beyond despair, we offered our wreckage to our Creator and were hopeful that joy might break through.

All we knew was that the Damoh police were determined to arrest Daddy. The superintendent of police claimed he was being forced to misuse his authority. He was harassing innocent people, and he knew exactly what he was doing. In retrospect, I realize that in those difficult moments, prayers were indeed our shield, protecting Daddy and our family. When our arms grew tired of being raised to the heavens, there were hundreds, even thousands, of arms lifted on our behalf. The overwhelming gratitude for these prayers will stay with me through eternity.

All this was taking place right before the elections, a time when the misuse of federal investigative agencies—the Enforcement Directorate (ED), Central Bureau of Investigation (CBI), and the Income Tax Department—seemed to escalate under the BJP government. Opposition parties claimed these agencies were weaponized to harass political rivals, especially during elections.

But why was Daddy being targeted? People were saying that there was a selective targeting of people who seem threatening to the BJP. But how was Daddy a threat? He stayed far away from politics, never aligning with any particular political party. We care about human beings not humanly created labels.

Still, it seemed that even the perception of being a threat to the BJP was enough. Some family friends had joined the BJP, but surely a political label didn't change one's heart, mind, or spirit. Or did it? Were we witnessing democratic backsliding in India? What our family faced certainly felt like an experience under fascism.

Daddy spent some time away from our home until tensions seemed to subside and the threat of being arrested diminished. But when he returned home, we were all more wary than ever, especially in the evenings. As the warmth of the day slipped into a cool dusk, and as the last streaks of sunlight stretched across the sky, the air grew still and quiet. That silence carried the weight of anticipation, of unspoken worries that lingered, waiting to be released or smoothed over.

Inside our home, we gathered around the table as we always did, holding onto routines as if they were anchors in a sea of uncertainty. Maa would set out the meal, each dish familiar, comforting, almost reverent.

She always embraced hospitality come what may, and she loved to feed us.

In that moment, we gave thanks to God and enjoyed the food and fellowship. There needed to be an intentionality to protect the sacred space of home especially in light of the circus that was brewing outside our boundary walls.

My brother would lighten the mood. "Lost another half percent body fat," he would announce while smiling and flexing his bicep playfully. We always laughed, grateful for the levity.

My husband would talk about his business trips to Dubai and America, asking the family when we wanted to plan our next family vacation. Dreaming about these vacations gave us something to look forward to as we hoped to rise above the chaos.

Maa and Daddy nudged Baabu. "So, champ, you'll be the next soccer star?"

"Baaba, you have another invitation to play in Spain," Lee said with pride. Baaba's face lit up, a grin spreading like the first rays of dawn. Mealtimes were special!

But the truth was more complex, shadowed by a darkness that was trying so desperately to cling to us even here in this seemingly safe space. But we were clinging onto God in whom "was life, and that life was the light of all mankind. The light shines in the darkness, and the darkness has not overcome it" (John 1:4–5 NIV).

Beyond the walls of our home a horrific story played out—a story of trials and turmoil that felt as relentless as a consuming tide. The office, which had once been my father's beacon for change, often felt like a tangled web of inquiries, ensnaring everyone involved in a haze of distraction when the staff was there to do meaningful work. Every morning, Daddy left with squared shoulders and a weight in his eyes as he faced yet another wave of inquiries, accusations, and fabricated scandals.

The police often showed up just to harass and intimidate without any reason other than to rehash things that had already been settled in the High Court in our favor. But the local officers were acting as though they wanted to keep bringing back the trauma on the "accused."

When the tensions were especially thick, the kids could sense the strange eeriness in the air and would sometimes ask, "Mama, why are people being mean to Papa when Papa is so kind to everyone?"

I made sure the children didn't have access to media, but they were surrounded by people who were talking. And they were old enough to understand that something was seriously wrong.

What is this place turning into? I thought.

My husband was often traveling overseas and didn't realize the extent of what was taking place in Damoh. None of us could have imagined. We hoped for the best, clinging to the fragile peace within the walls of our home, but these petty goons kept threatening us kept saying, "there is pressure from higher authorities" and that "high level people are involved." What was with all the mob mentality? What was with all the defamation and oppression? My children were being affected!

My mind drifted to stories of other families and figures whose lives had been irrevocably altered by scandal and resistance. There were leaders who had once held the public's favor, only to be betrayed, discredited, or driven into exile when their truths clashed with popular belief. *Scandals are strange beasts*, I thought, *carrying the power to strip people of belonging, to unravel the threads of identity.*

Watching my father shoulder the burden, I wondered how he endured it. Was it worth it? In my heart, I knew the answer, but it didn't make the weight any lighter.

One evening, as we sipped on chai, Maa reached across the space between us and rested her hand gently on mine. "Remember this, Beta," she murmured, her voice a soft balm against the encroaching dusk. "Remember that there is beauty even when life is hard." Even though sometimes I find Maa's focus on the positive hard to comprehend, her words settled into my heart like a seed, a quiet truth that would anchor me in the days to come. For despite the shadows we faced, there remained pockets of light, glimmers of hope that sparkled through the darkness. I was grateful for moments of reprieve that gave me a welcomed break from the turbulence. These moments were reminders that beauty still existed beyond our immediate troubles, that nature had its own silent healing power—that there are still spaces where the symphony of life played on without interruption.

Every time I returned to Damoh, home felt less familiar, more like a place that was saying, "Your time here is nearing the end." No one wants to hear that from their home, the place that was once a place of sanctuary.

Each day brought with it fresh challenges and rumors that clawed at our sense of safety as though they sought to unravel the sanctuary we tried to build. Regardless of what the day showed us, every night we would gather and each take a moment to name something we were grateful for. It was a ritual that anchored us and reminded us that despite everything we had each other. This practice, simple as it was, became a discipline that built strength. It was how we remembered who we were even when the world seemed intent on rewriting our story.

The return to India was an act of love. I always thought my dad had an irrational love for India. My husband, kids, and I came back to India carrying our hopes in both hands, palms wide open, ready to offer whatever we could. My parents always worked in India with a passion that said that maybe if we worked hard enough, loved fiercely enough, something beautiful would take root. And it did. Generational wounds were healed; cycles of poverty and sickness were broken; hope was restored in many broken spaces. But India needs leaders with renovated hearts if the nation wants to truly heal from its hurt and colonial hangover. Otherwise, it will always be like the wounded and weary lover who is suspicious of kindness and sometimes lashes out and other times recoils when a well-meaning partner reaches out with genuine love.

Before we arrived, we worked with my parents to help bring the Oxygen Plant to the mission hospital during the pandemic. During the pandemic, Oxygen plants played an important role in saving lives because healthcare facilities were running out of oxygen in India. There was an escalating demand for oxygen cylinders but the supply chain couldn't keep up. Because of the oxygen supply plant, the mission hospital wasn't depending on oxygen cylinders to ensure every patient was guaranteed sufficient oxygen to heal from their respiratory challenges. This was my father's idea to ensure that there was an oxygen plant at the mission hospital so that the people in and around Damoh didn't have to face the same challenges as the rest of India. Our family prayerfully worked together to help gather resources for this facility. Carrying the legacy of generations, we poured out our energy as a labor of love. But now this felt like a dysfunctional dance.

There is a cycle that jaded hearts slip into. A place where hope becomes dangerous and love unbearable, where it feels safer to stay underdeveloped and broken than risk being made whole—especially by people who don't call themselves Hindus but choose to live as followers of Christ. But to maintain one's own health one needs to establish boundaries and get out of that dysfunctional relationship, the codependency that comes with unhealthy patriotism masked as nationalism. There comes a time when enough is enough.

I loved. We gave. My parents gave five decades of their lives for their country! Our children were affected by the trauma of not knowing if our loved ones are safe. Still, we pressed on, hoped, and believed for as long as we could. That is its own kind of grace.

But now is the time to heal.

I never felt more proud to be an American. For the first time this recognition set in deeply. This land never forced me to choose between my Indian roots and the soil beneath my feet in the United States. This is where I was finally free to tell my story as I experienced it. Being born here, gave me room to stretch those roots—to honor my unique history and heritage and ask my own questions.

Being connected to this land, gave my family an opportunity to heal—a path many are never privileged enough to travel. We can fully embrace our Indian ethos without apology. Free to speak multiple languages, free to celebrate faith, family, and tradition. Free to tell my story from my standpoint. As for my parents, who are senior citizens, at this stage of life, part of their healing is to be forced to reevaluate their sense of identity, home, and belonging. America gave us the space to carry our heritage not as a burden, but as a blessing.

7

Hanging on to the Good

There are still flashbacks. Flickers of memory, of that thick, oppressive time we lived through in Damoh—especially between 2022 and 2024—when air turned to ash and even the trees in the garden stood in disbelief.

One night, as the house folded into silence like a letter no one dared open, I found myself sitting across the dining table across Daddy. The weight of the day settled into the silence between us. He thought I was not paying attention, sitting there casually at the end of the day, painting my nails. But I could see the weariness in his eyes, the unspoken burden he carried. I longed to ask him, *Do you ever regret it?* But I didn't want to sound brazen and insensitive. There was no reason to rupture the calm of that moment. The silence helped me hold the words back as I didn't want to disturb the peace.

But then, as I often do, I couldn't hold back and spoke my mind. "Just let them burn in their own fury. Don't hold onto this place filled with such petty people with their small, twisted hearts."

He looked at me, his gaze unwavering. "No," he replied. There was always a steady fire in Daddy's eyes that never went out. "Because I believe in what we're doing. And I believe that if we hold on, if we stand firm, there will be light at the end of this."

It was a belief that had carried him through, and in that moment, I decided to leave it at that. We all needed to cope, and if that thought, that kind of belief—pure, clean, completely unreasonable—helped him in that moment, I wasn't going to argue. So, I left it there. If that hope was his survival, who was I to tear it apart?

As I reflected on our situation, stories of resilience, of families who had faced betrayals and losses yet found ways to hold on, filled my mind. There are stories passed down of people who held on through betrayal, through exile, through fire. And in some twisted way, we had become a footnote in that story. But we will never be okay living in someone else's rewriting of history. Our struggle felt connected to the trials of those who had come before us. We were, in a sense, living our own chapter in a history that stretched far beyond us.

At home, our family remained our greatest strength. We were each other's sanctuary. Each member held a unique role. Each of us was a piece of the foundation that kept us steady. My brother and sister-in-law, with their light-hearted banter, reminded us to laugh. Joy refused to die. Lee, with his quiet strength, anchored us in hope. The children, bless them, with their innocence and joy embodied resilience. My sisters and brother-in-law, with their deep care, were often unaware of what was going on but were always anchored in prayer. And my parents, with their unwavering resolve, reminded us that through it all

God is at work. Our closeness remained a safe space for all of us, showing us what it meant to endure. Back when we were in Damoh, there were nights when the weight felt almost too heavy to bear, but as we sat together, sharing our gratitude and our fears, we felt the strength of our bond. We were more than a family; we remained a haven in a world that seemed intent on breaking us.

In the end, it was my father's words that kept us moving forward. "We will keep going," he said one evening, his voice steady, his gaze filled with a quiet determination. We nodded and a silent promise passed between us—a commitment to each other, to the life we had built, to the love that held us together.

In our shared struggles, in our laughter and gratitude, we had found something unbreakable, a strength that no scandal, no trial, could ever take away. In that strength I found a joy that was real, grounded, unwavering. And so I had reason to give thanks every day!

It wasn't enough that we were persecuted from the outside. The threats weren't just out there in the streets. We increasingly suspected that there were people close to us, in our very midst, who were willing to betray us. That is how fascism works. It seeps. It whispers. It turns servants into informants and neighbors into spies. It doesn't knock; it slithers in through cracks in trust.

There were those who had sat at our tables at my grandparents' home, who'd enjoyed Maa's hospitality, who had hugged Daddy at weddings, and now they were working with those who wanted to destroy my father and the legacy of my grandfather. They were smiling with one face and reporting with the other.

Power, once it is seized, has a way of shifting the landscape. It takes root in places most vulnerable—within families, communities, and institutions—exploiting trust and sowing discord. And so it was with us. People in power began gathering information from those close to the family. These people were feigning loyalty while conspiring in the shadows. At first, I refused to believe it. It seemed too cruel, too intimate. But the truth began to show its face. You can only hide rot for so long.

We should not have been surprised. Politically, fascism breeds fear, resentment, and division, often leading to violence and persecution. Personally, it festers in relationships, turning allies into traitors. The nostalgia of the imili trees had faded. The focus was on here and now.

When Daddy and Uncle Dave sold a plot of land that they inherited from my grandfather, small men with smaller dreams saw their chance to strike. The buyer used the land for a small business, but rather than go after the new owner, the petty goons filed an FIR against Daddy and Uncle Dave. Because that is how cowards fight: sideways and in the shadows.

The court saw through it. The judge ruled in my father's favor on September 30, 2022. The judge recognized my father as a man of service, and called out the goons for targeting a senior citizen—Uncle Dave—who had barely survived a triple bypass surgery the year before.

But power doesn't like losing.

Hanging on to the Good

The day after Daddy's first victory in the High Court, the persecution intensified. Someone slaughtered a cow and left the carcass on my father's office campus. In the state of Madhya Pradesh, where Domah was located, the punishment for killing a cow is harsher than the punishment for killing a human being. Whoever was doing this was taking a great risk - they were baiting blood.

Thankfully, we weren't in Damoh at the time. Before we even knew about it, Priyank Kanoongo, a man whose name should be synonymous with trauma, tweeted about it. This was the same man who had terrorized the female staff and kids at the children's home, and who had weaponized his position at the National Child Protection Agency to target Muslims and Christians alike – apparently he had been promoted to the Human Rights Commission.

Human rights, they said. Human. Rights.

The mobs came next, roaring again in the streets. Burning effigies again as they had done after August 15, 2022. Shouting slurs. These thugs were hired goons, faceless agents of chaos, who were yet again not arrested. Journalists—once thought of as truth-tellers—colluded with them, calling my dad and Uncle Dave *chor* (Hindi for "thief") in the local newspapers.

Thankfully, as this dangerous scenario unfolded, my family and I weren't in Damoh. We were in a remote area celebrating the court victory and hoping to return home soon, naively believing that the nightmare was over.

But this ongoing petty drama forced us to live like gypsies yet again. We were living out of suitcases, unable to use our phones. We were disconnected from the internet, and our schedules were inconsistent. My daughter, a straight-A student, cried in frustration because she couldn't keep up with her home-schooling. It wasn't that the curriculum was too challenging, but we didn't always have reliable internet access. Our children were being affected.

In the middle of all this, Lee and I made the painful decision to send our children to boarding school. A decision I had once sworn never to make. My parents had sent me to boarding school on the foothills of the Himalayas, and I used to tell them they had conveniently outsourced parenting. But now I was faced with this impossible math of love and survival. I never wanted to send my kids off to boarding school. But now, I had much more compassion for the complexity of the decision my parents had made when I was a child—and the decision Lee and I now faced. As we left our children at the school, we kissed their foreheads and reassured them we'd always be together for birthdays and special occasions. Even though the school offered a safe and nurturing environment, it all felt forced and unnatural. Nothing felt whole.

I felt torn between my duties as a daughter, wife, and mother. The world in which I was raising my children was vastly different from my husband's Midwestern American upbringing, and even more distant from Damoh, Madhya Pradesh, where my parents had chosen to live. It was impossible to reconcile these worlds into a cohesive, integrated whole. There were scattered fragments of who I was supposed to be in the face of all this and who I used to be. There was no map, just prayer. Just breath.

Exhaustion crept in as, not feeling fully at home, I felt a responsibility to call the land of my forefathers my home. It felt nothing like home anymore. I grew more thankful for the home we had established by the Rocky Mountains. But couldn't bear the thought of leaving India not knowing if our family was safe. The decision to flee a homeland is usually a last resort, as potential refugees hold onto hope for as long as possible, reluctant to leave until they have no choice. There is a deep internal conflict as they weigh the risks of staying against the perils of leaving everything behind: their homes, communities, meaningful work they've built their entire lives. Most refugees don't flee because they want to. They flee because the ground beneath them becomes something they no longer recognize.

We hadn't yet crossed boarders, but we were already feeling displaced. In some ways my parents seemed unwilling to acknowledge the rising storm. In other ways they appeared to be seeking shelter. My mother, a fierce prayer warrior, had been saying for months, "Every time I pray, I get this strong feeling that we shouldn't be here, especially in 2024."

As the eldest daughter, I tried to stay strong even through emotionally and mentally, the rising storm was assaulting us all. We watched truth go up in flames, along with our sense of safety.

As for my family and me, we were witnessing the breakdown of social structures before our very eyes and already feeling displaced as we watched the destruction unfold. And through it all, we did what survivors do: we held onto each other. We thanked God for each day—each blessing—every glimpse of goodness.

And still the tall palm trees, the ancient tamarind trees, every new rose bush in the garden stood. Silent witnesses to a family fighting to stay rooted.

8

The Shadow of Fascism

Despite multiple court orders clearing his name, the harassment of my father didn't stop like a rising tide. The prolonged trauma needed to stop.

Government agencies began conducting weekly inspections at the children's home, hunting—beneath files, inside fridges, under beds—for any reason to shut it down. The walls held the echoes of sobs—children and staff left traumatized after one especially brutal visit in November 2022. The man who led that raid, Priyank Kanoongo, wasn't just cruel. He was calculated. He had become their tormentor. His voice was acidic. His accusations were rehearsed and baseless but aggressive and cruel. His disregard for women and children was palpable. His abusive language was caught on camera on multiple occasions. How had such a person been given power?

The children's home had raised generations of abandoned children who were now doctors, engineers, nurses, teachers, and parents. And yet, this place of refuge was now under siege. The attacks weren't just physical. They were bureaucratic and psychological, designed to exhaust, disorient, and shame.

By 2023, the assault widened.

There were threats to vandalize the mission hospital. Some extremists began loudly and publicly saying that Christians shouldn't be entrusted with such an institution, suggesting it should be seized by the government. Some people confused the work of other uncles with the work of my father because they shared the same last name. The baseless accusations and harassment were relentless. Even with divine strength, a human being can only face so much. There are implications of prolonged trauma, but through it all God somehow shielded our joy.

The institution my father had helped establish faced 167 inquiries between August 2022 and August 2023. Ninety-six of those were in-person inspections, where staff and leaders were interrogated, and seventy-one inquiries demanded exhaustive written explanations for every department—the main office, Children's Home, and Nursing College. Thanks to the power of prayers, many inspectors arrived as skeptics but left as friends, recognizing the integrity and excellence of the work. Each staff member stood firm, driven by the conviction that we must remain faithful to God's calling, but the wounds of this scrutiny would take time to heal. The emotional and mental trauma inflicted by these constant intrusions left deep scars, especially on the children, who lost their sense of home and security. They began to fear what a knock on the door might mean.

Then came a huge blow.

They succeeded in shutting down the children's home in Damoh. The same home that had housed the

The Shadow of Fascism

abandoned. They asked for records of children abandoned in 2006—children who had since been legally adopted through the Central Adoption Resource Authority. But by law those records were to be destroyed two years after adoption. It was a trap. They knew it. We knew it. But the outcome was the same. Children were torn away from what they had always known to be their home and shelter.

What kind of people use the lives of orphans for political purposes?

The attacks were meant to shatter not just buildings but the will of those inside them. The rise of extremism in India was no longer a matter of political leanings; it was seeping into the soul of society. Hate speech against Christian leaders was normalized, even admired in some circles. And mob violence followed, as it always does, like smoke after fire.

In April 2023, the Supreme Court of India became concerned and recognized hate speech against Christian leaders and institutions as a catalyst for mob violence against religious minorities. It was a flicker of hope—a signal that someone, somewhere, was watching. That the lamp of justice still burned, even if merely flickering. But the court's directives were ignored by those in power. Men like Kanoongo kept tweeting, kept defaming, kept fueling the fire with impunity.

The cancellation of the children's home's registration was just one example of the structural cruelty my parents faced. The registration—first granted in 2006—had been renewed in 2012 and again in 2018. The application for renewal was submitted on January 18, 2023, for both boys' and girls' homes. In response, the district officer asked to separate the applications, which was done on February 6.

On August 14, 2023, the registration was terminated for both homes by the Women and Child Development Department, Ministry, Ballabh Bhawan, Bhopal. The institution in Damoh was finally notified on September 5 by the District Program Officer, Women and Child Development, Damoh.

The High Court, recognizing the injustice, intervened on September 15 and ordered that the home be allowed to continue to operate. But then another hearing was set for September 25.

This is just one example of how the structural harassment compounded the challenges faced by the institution.

The process was like running a marathon underwater.

Exhausting to read, yes.

Excruciating to live through.

Resources bled. Emotions frayed. Some days we had to stay more intentional about taking deep breaths between hearings and inspections and whispers of new accusations. And yet, in that chaos, the judiciary stood like the final pillar in a house collapsing in a storm—not perfect but still standing.

Meanwhile, the vendetta raged in plain view. Mr. Vivek Tankha, a respected senior advocate and an honorable member of the upper house of parliament, told me, "I have never seen such a vendetta against one person the way I have seen it carried out against your dad." He stood by my father when it felt like the world was against us.

The Shadow of Fascism

On September 16, 2023, the Hindi-language daily newspaper *Dainik Bhaskar* published a headline:

> CHILDREN LYING UNCONSCIOUS IN AN INTOXICATED STATE AT THE DAMOH RAILWAY STATION.

Did Kanoongo send a team to investigate those children?
Did the state care?
That same week, another report:

> HUNDREDS OF CHILDREN OF EKLAVYA RESIDENTIAL SCHOOL FELL ILL. A MASS FOOD POISONING IN A GOVERNMENT-RUN INSTITUTION.

No raids. No FIRs. No Twitter storms. No tears televised.
Where then was the scrutiny?
Where was the outrage?
Were these people measuring the value of children by the institutions they belonged to rather than their worth as human beings?
During the same period, thousands of Indian teenagers died by suicide, victims of bureaucratic corruption surrounding the National Eligibility cum Entrance Test, a mandatory entrance exam for aspiring medical and dental students in India. Children who dreamed of becoming doctors, crushed by a system rigged against them. There wasn't a single statement of sympathy, let alone empathy from the education minister. He remained unmoved. He

was reappointed to the same post in Modi's cabinet after the 2024 elections.

The world watched. And then looked away.

When the world falls silent, the cries of the oppressed are swallowed whole.

But we heard them.

We still hear them.

This is the very reason that God's work doesn't falter. Across India—a nation strained by protests, riots, corruption, and silence—bold leaders continue to serve in clinics, in schools, in shelters. They quietly and steadily serve while being slandered by those who have never served anyone but themselves.

The aim of the violence, the surveillance, and the bureaucratic strangulation was to silence us.

But we are not silent.

And we are not alone.

In India and across the world there are people of conscience. People who see through the noise and recognize the truth beneath it. Who believe that dignity is not a luxury but a right. That justice is not partisan but sacred.

What they did to the children's home in 2023 they would do to the mission hospital in 2025. Misinformation. False accusations. Grotesque efforts. A vendetta to vilify Christians and their efforts.

This struggle was not just about one home or some court cases. It was about belonging. About identity. About whether there is room in this new India for those who love differently, serve differently.

We believe there is.

The Shadow of Fascism

And so we continue.
We fight.
We pray.
We endure.
Because the story of our lives does not end with fear.
It moves forward with faith.
It progresses with light.
It goes on through eternity with love that refuses to be erased.

9

A Christmas Message of Hope?

It was the winter of 2023, and the nights came early. Even before the sky could dim to grey, shadows settled into the corners of the house like old memories—familiar, patient, waiting. We no longer gathered at Dada-Dadi's house. That place, once so full of life, was now left as an empty, eerie relic. But Maa and Daddy had built a beautiful enclave for our family. Just as Dada and Dadi's home was marked by the memories of the tamarind trees around it, Maa and Daddy's home was surrounded by palm trees whose branches swayed gently in the cold breeze. And the air, as it had done so many years before, carried with it the smell of earth, incense, and quiet unease.

Around Christmas time, Prime Minister Narendra Modi hosted some Christian leaders at his residence. He spoke of Jesus with reverence. His voice was measured, warm even. He praised the Christian community's role in India's freedom movement. He mentioned Christian schools, hospitals, and acts of service scattered across the subcontinent like oil laps in a long corridor. He said that the teachings of Christ remained vital to India's progress.

A Christmas Message of Hope?

It was a well-constructed gesture, a balm carefully applied. And it landed on a bruised, aching body.

There is something about elegant words spoken in wounded spaces. They shimmer at first. They offer the illusion of healing like an open wound beneath a bandage. Many listened. Some hoped. Others turned away, unwilling to risk disappointment again. In a place where gestures are often dissonant from realities on the ground, that flicker of hope can dim quickly.

It was like the trees in the garden were holding their breath. Those trees that once felt so alive with the laughter of cousins and rustling branches, now just stood there like quiet sentinels. There was a stillness, not just in the garden but in the hearts of many who had once known this land as home. And yet, inside me, there was a disquiet—not cynicism, not yet. Just a quiet ache like the feeling that lingers when someone you love says the right thing after having said the wrong thing for far too long. You want to believe them. You want the warmth of their words to be real. But trust, once shaken, does not return with a single gesture.

Tears welled up as I remembered sitting by the garden wall, tea growing cold in my hand, thinking of the old Christmases at Dada and Dadi's house. I remembered the swell of voices as people from every faith gathered in celebration not in conversion or protest but in joy. Hindus, Muslims, Sikhs, Jains, atheists, Christians all filled the halls and spilled into the verandah, singing carols, sharing food, laughing under the strings of fairy lights. That was our India. That was the India I wished my children could witness.

So, when Modi stood before the cameras—ever so composed—and spoke of peace and Jesus and national unity, I wanted to believe that perhaps, just perhaps, there was still space in this country for the kind of India I had known. But memory is a fragile thing when it comes up against the machinery of power.

Because in Manipur, Christmas lights were dimmed by the smoke of burning churches. In Madhya Pradesh and Chhattisgarh pastors were arrested on dubious charges. In village after village families were told to renounce their faith or face consequences. Faith-based NGOs that had fed the hungry and clothed the poor found their bank accounts frozen, their licenses revoked, their mission questioned.

And so, while Modi spoke of harmony, many of us sat in silence, wrestling with a deeper grief: The grief of being gaslit by the leaders of our motherland. The grief of watching one's identity reduced to suspicion. The grief of wondering if your very faith, passed down by generations who loved and served this land, had become a liability.

For many Christians in India, Modi's words felt like sunlight passing through glass: bright but not warm. When reconciliation is needed, words alone are not enough. True healing demands repentance, justice, and a return to truth.

I reflected on what the Bible says in 1 Samuel 16:7—"People look at the outward appearance, but the LORD looks at the heart." So we listened, not just to what was said but to what was left unsaid. Not just to the speech but to the silences that followed. Because even as Modi spoke of peace, the soil still bore the weight of blood, tears, and ashes.

When churches were being burned and Christian homes destroyed, especially in Manipur, activists called it one of the worst communal tragedies since Gujarat in 2002 and Kandhamal in 2008. The violence was not random. It was targeted. Calculated. Rooted in decades of unhealed fractures.

In Rajasthan, Uttar Pradesh, Madhya Pradesh, Chhattisgrah—states shaped by Hindutva governance—the space to live and worship freely has continued to shrink. Anti-conversion laws cloaked in the language of protection have become tools of persecution. Christian institutions have their registrations revoked. There is no due process, no transparency. Just letters, mockery, and public vilification of religious minority leaders.

It wasn't always like this.

India's Christian community has long served without spectacle. From Mother Teresa's sisters to tribal pastors, from elite academic institutions to lowly rural clinics Christians have lived out their faith not in slogans but in service. They have touched the untouchables, welcomed the orphaned, and offered healing without condition. Their reward? Vilification. Accusation. Exclusion. They aren't safe in their own homeland.

The roots of this betrayal run deeper than any one government. They stretch into the trauma of colonialism, into the scars of the Emergency, into the uneasy inheritance of a post-Partition identity, when people sharing the same DNA were forced to be divided into India and Pakistan.

India's leaders have often led from a place of unresolved pain, clutching at power, fearing difference, policing dissent. But true and godly leadership requires more than strength. It requires heart, perhaps a renovated heart.

So many people face no ramifications for making bold, public hate speeches against religious minorities. Meanwhile, Rahul Gandhi, the face of the opposition, was sentenced to two years in prison for defaming the prime minister. It took the Supreme Court's intervention to restore his right to serve in parliament. And that same court—India's highest judicial body—remains one of the last fragile safeguards of democracy. But even it is haunted by the pressures of majoritarian sentiment.

Opposition leaders, activists, and journalists continue to be hounded. Members of the Aam Aadmi Party have faced arrests under questionable circumstances. Voices calling for transparency, for equity, for environmental justice, or gender rights, are often branded anti-national.

Meanwhile, those who inflame religious hatred often walk free.

This is what structural violence looks like. It does not always explode; it seeps. It becomes normal. Expected. Unnoticed. It is the silence after a raid, the absence of funding, the hesitation in a pastor's voice. It is the fear that creeps in where joy once lived.

And yet, as believers, we remain rooted. Because our faith is not in policies, but in God's promises.

In Vedic literature, *dharma* is not nationalism; it is virtue, a way of life anchored in truth, in compassion, in responsibility. In the book of James, we are told that "faith without works is dead" (James 2:26). Both teachings—one from the Hindu tradition and one from the Bible—point to the truth that religion must never be hollow. It must transform not just preach. It must liberate not bind.

Religion is not the problem. Weaponized religion is.

We cannot let sacred texts become shields for cruelty. We cannot allow the memory of Muslim poets, Christian missionaries, Buddhist monks, and secular thinkers to be erased. They, too, are India. They, too, are the spirit of the land.

When a land is steeped in spirituality, its people need to return to the core, not performance, or spectacle, but love, service, and mercy. One day we will all stand before God. As Jesus said: "I was hungry and you gave me something to eat, I was a stranger and you invited me in… Truly I tell you, whatever you did for one of the least of these brothers and sisters of mine, you did for me" (Matthew 25:35–36, 40).

We will not be judged by our party affiliations or last names, our linguistic loyalties or our cultural orthodoxy. We will be judged by love.

Even Jesus, a practicing Jew, challenged the religious elites of his time. He exposed their hypocrisy. He called out those who wielded faith as a performance. He asked us to want not in fear but in truth.

So yes, when Modi extended the Christmas greetings, I did not reject them. I received them but with caution, with prayer, with the hope that this might be the beginning of something real. But I also held those words up to the light of lived experience. Because gratitude, to be lasting, must be more than seasonal sentiment. It must become an action. A posture. A way of seeing the world.

Gratitude that does not recognize suffering is not gratitude. It is performance.

And yet, light shines brighter in the darkness and the darkness cannot overcome the light (John 1:5).

In every village there is still someone feeding a child. In every hospital, a nurse prays before her shift. In every broken church, a congregation sings. The candles are still lit. The carols are still sung. The story is still told. The story of a child born not in a palace but in a manger. Not to conquer but to redeem. Not to divide but to heal. Allowing each individual the freedom to choose their journey with God.

So we celebrate Christmas, not because all is well but because God came anyway.

The trees still stand, swaying in the breeze. The wind still whispers through their leaves. And though the world beneath them has changed, they have not fallen.

Neither will we.

10

Finding Stillness in Sant Cugat

It was one of those moments where the present becomes more vivid than the past or future, as though life itself were inviting you to pause and breathe deeply.

That's what Sant Cugat del Vallès, Spain, did to me. This quiet little town, tucked away from the hustle and bustle of Barcelona, enveloped us in its serenity. It wasn't just the charming streets or the lush green parks. It was a feeling, almost tangible, that whispered *You can rest here!*

We had come because of our son's soccer program, a whirlwind of practices, games, and travel schedules that often left us running from one commitment to the next. Yet somehow, as we stepped off the taxi into Sant Cugat, the world seemed to slow down.

The town's rhythm wasn't dictated by urgency but by intention. The cobblestones underfoot, the centuries-old monastery standing in quiet grace, the locals chatting in hushed tones over coffee all spoke of a life that didn't demand attention but invited it.

Herman Hesse's words came to mind almost instinctively: "Within you, there is a stillness and a sanctuary to which you can retreat at any time and be yourself." In Sant Cugat I found that sanctuary—not just in the town itself but within. The stillness of this place mirrored something I'd forgotten about myself, something easily lost amidst the chaos of life as a parent, an advocate, and a dreamer. The hustle and bustle, the trauma of India was creating a layer of callus somewhere where it should never be. Sant Cugat was that warm soak in water before the callus could be removed.

The soccer program was, of course, the reason we were there. Our son, with his boundless energy and love for the game, had brought us to places we might never have visited otherwise. But as I watched him run across the field, laughing and playing with the kind of joy only children seem to know, I realized it wasn't just his passion for soccer that was shaping him. It was the places, the people, and the experiences along the way.

Sant Cugat was leaving its mark—not only on him but on all of us. We needed a fresh new perspective and a reminder of what is a beautiful and healthy rhythm of life, of togetherness.

Lee and I found ourselves walking through the town after practice one evening, our daughter happily recounting stories from her day. The streets glowed under the soft golden light of lampposts, and the air carried a hint of pine from the surrounding hills. We stumbled upon a small café, where we sat for what felt like hours savoring simple yet perfect plates of tapas and goblets of soothing richness.

"'This is where I want to grow old," I said aloud, the words escaping almost without thought. Lee looked at me, then at the town around us, and nodded. Neither of us needed to explain.

There's something about Sant Cugat that made you feel as though you belonged, even as a visitor. Perhaps it was the way life there. The people seemed to value connection over convenience. Or maybe it was the natural beauty of the place, the way the mountains cradled the town, offering both protection and inspiration. Or maybe it was the monastery being a central part of its beauty and artistic inspiration! Whatever it was, I knew that if soccer continued to guide our family's journey, I wouldn't mind if it eventually led us back here for good.

For now, though, we were content to be present. Sant Cugat had given us more than a respite from the chaos of life. It had reminded us that stillness is not just a place but a way of being. And for that, I was grateful.

This place had already lulled us into a sense of tranquility, but Barcelona brought a vibrancy and richness that perfectly complemented the whole experience. I love that it flows as a city of contrasts, where centuries-old traditions dance alongside modern energy.

And on our daughter's fourteenth birthday, it became the backdrop for a day that perfectly reflected her—a delightful blend of history, art, and sweetness.

"Happy birthday, Babypie," Lee said with a grin as Princess-pie rushed out of her room, her excitement barely contained. It was a nickname we had given her as a toddler, one that had stuck despite her teenage protests. She rolled her eyes playfully but couldn't hide her smile. To celebrate, we decided to embark on a chocolate tour, a plan that seemed to combine all her interests into one perfect day. Her growing love for history and art had been a joy to witness. She absorbed stories of the past as though they were living things, weaving them effortlessly into her understanding of the world. Add to that her budding appreciation for culinary arts, and Chocolate Amatller was the obvious choice.

Nestled in the heart of Barcelona, Amatller House was far more than a home for one of Europe's oldest chocolate brands. Designed by the renowned Josep Puig i Cadafalch, the building stands as a masterpiece of Catalan modernism—a style that seemed to transition gracefully from Gothic architecture while embracing something entirely new. Its intricate façade, with stained glass and whimsical details that hinted at the creativity of the era, drew us in. The tour felt like stepping back in time.

As we wandered through rooms adorned with art nouveau elegance, we learned about the history of chocolate in Europe. It was fascinating to hear how this once-exotic delicacy played a pivotal role in diplomacy, becoming a symbol of refinement and power. We learned that beyond its political significance, chocolate influenced the social and cultural fabric of countless societies.

Why couldn't we have such sweet influences shaping our world today? I couldn't help but get lost in the romanticism of it all!

We tasted chocolate in some of its oldest forms, from the bitter drinks of the Mayans to the refined confections of nineteenth-century Europe. Babypie listened intently, asking questions about how trade and colonization impacted its history—a reminder of her ability to see the world with both curiosity and empathy.

"This place is amazing," she said, her eyes alight with wonder as she sampled a piece of dark chocolate infused with orange zest. "It's like a museum, a chocolate shop, and an art gallery all in one!"

Lee, ever the thoughtful father, had researched every detail of the experience, ensuring it would be something she'd treasure. As I watched the tour guide explain the intricacies of the building's architecture to her, I felt a swell of gratitude for the way Lee nurtured our children's passions.

The day ended with a small celebration back at our apartment, where we shared stories from the tour and laughed over how much chocolate we'd consumed. As I reflected on the day, I couldn't help but feel a deep sense of gratitude, not just for the experience but for the young woman our little princess was becoming. Her curiosity, her joy, her ability to find meaning in even the smallest details—these were gifts that enriched our family in ways I couldn't put into words.

That night, as we tucked her into bed, I whispered, "Happy birthday, my sweet girl. Watching you explore and grow is one of the greatest gifts God has given me." And it is true. Whether in the quiet of Sant Cugat or the liveliness of Barcelona, or in the hills of Kodaikanal, my daughter's spirit brought a light that made every place feel more meaningful. It hurt to think that we were missing so many glimpses while she was in boarding school, and she was just hiding her pain, trying to understand that we were trying the best we knew. We were all trying. But we needed to get on with life.

The future seemed as rich and full as the chocolate we'd tasted—a blend of sweetness, depth, and endless possibility. Spain had been a sanctuary—a place where stillness and joy intertwined seamlessly, offering a reprieve we hadn't realized we desperately needed. Barcelona added layers of discovery and sweetness to the memories, culminating in our baby's birthday celebration, where history, art, and chocolate mirrored her passions and curiosities. It was a trip I wished could stretch indefinitely, a dream I didn't want to wake from.

But reality has a way of intruding.

As we packed our bags, preparing to return to India, I felt a pang of longing, an ache to head in the opposite direction. A part of me wished we were returning to the majestic Rockies, to the familiar embrace of the mountains and the rhythms of a life Lee and I had once called our own. But the thought was unthinkable. How could I consider retreating to tranquility when, as a senior citizen, Daddy's very life was under threat, and Maa no longer knew who she could trust? Was this care or codependency? I no longer knew.

Maa and Daddy had been our rock. They had stood beside Lee and me through every season, every transition—long before Lee and I were even dating. They had been there for the births of both our children, pouring out their love, support, and generosity in ways only they could. Their home in Damoh had always been more than a house; it was a refuge. A place where we could return to gain perspective, to feel held and supported no matter what storms we faced.

Now, it was our turn. In their time of need, how could we leave them? And yet, the decision to stay in India carried its own burden. Protecting my children while being there for my parents meant making a heart-wrenching choice: Lee and I would have to drop the kids off at boarding school after we returned to India. It felt so jarring and unnatural! The flight back was heavy, the conversations subdued.

We arrived in Tamil Nadu and, with great reluctance, left the children in the misty hills of their school. I tried to keep my composure, assuring them this was temporary, but my heart broke as I hugged them goodbye. Every parent dreams of giving their children a secure, unbroken sense of home, and this felt like anything but that. But we try our best with the situations at hand, and that is all we can do.

Lee and I then made our way back to Madhya Pradesh. Traveling to Damoh felt interminable, the weight of what lay ahead pressing down on us. Lee had meetings in Dubai, so he left the next morning, and I found myself alone with my thoughts. And then, the welcome I had dreaded came crashing down. That same morning Lee left, news arrived that the local bureaucrats, working hand in glove with local goons, had fabricated a FIR against my brother. It had been filed at 4:00 a.m. by an uneducated, unemployed former employee of the mission hospital. A man who had worked there for fourteen years, resigned, and now sought to exploit our family for financial gain.

The details blurred in my mind as I tried to process it all—the absurdity of the accusations, the malice with which this case had been orchestrated. This was our reality now: a daily battle against forces intent on dismantling everything Daddy had built, everything the family stood for and held dear! Thankfully, the judiciary kept on upholding justice time and time again. The judges could see though the vendetta against us and that is what set the judges apart from the petty goons who kept trying to manipulate, dominate, and intimidate well-meaning people.

The magic of Sant Cugat, the sweetness of my baby's birthday, the serenity of quiet streets—all of it felt like a distant dream, fading rapidly as the harshness of life in India demanded attention. Yet even in the chaos, I clung to the memory of those moments, drawing strength from the stillness I had found within.

Sant Cugat had reminded me that sanctuary isn't always about a place. Sometimes, it's about a state of being, a place within where we can retreat when the storms rage. As we faced the challenges ahead, I carried that lesson close, praying it would somehow bring sustenance in the midst of the battles yet to come.

11

US Citizens Unlawfully Detained

That first week of August 2024, will be forever burned into my memory. A searing unshakable stretch of time where every moment felt as if it was unfolding under a sky the color of unshed tears. The superintendent of police in Damoh did not want to be seen with my father, but he agreed to meet with me. He seemed respectful and understanding of our family's situation, but at the same time he was measured with his words. I spoke plainly, without accusation. My message to him was a simple request to let our family live peacefully.

If the people of Damoh no longer wanted my parents there, then I didn't want them to remain in a place that had become unsafe. At this stage in their lives, they deserved the dignity of a peaceful transition. God blessed us with a home and loved ones both in India and in the United States. Why cling to danger when sanctuary had been so faithfully provided?

The superintendent of police could have helped. He could have refused to entertain the slander and baseless claims spewing from the mouths of small-minded men. Instead, he spoke of his limitations, of pressures. Pressures from where? From whom? Why this obsession with arresting my father? Why permit lies to be hurled like stones while standing silent?

He sat there feigning sympathy. A big sign promoting loving and protecting his country hung front and center in his office. I wanted to believe that he understood our situation and would stand with us, but the days ahead would reveal that indeed this man was acting "under pressure." But still the question lingered: Who was pressuring him? Who was feeding him the misinformation against us? Why was he so hell bent to arrest my father, and why was he allowing hate-filled lies to spread against us? The High Court had issued him a show cause notice, a formal request to justify his actions. To this day, I have not heard of his reply!

"Something big is happening on August 6," he had warned me there in his office. His eyes were steady and his voice was low. "My hands are tied. I have my limitations. If you want to stop it, go to the chief minister."

We tried. No response.

Sure enough, the morning of August 6 police officers swarmed my father's office. They arrived like a storm, trying to intimidate and harass without a warrant.

We usually had lunch together, but that afternoon Daddy had still not returned home by 3:00 p.m. He had not eaten all day. He hadn't taken his daily medications. When I went to his office to check on him, the scene was surreal.

Police officers, lawyers, journalists, people from the city were all hovering. Some were supportive. Others were there with the intent to harass, to provoke, to press, to push. Why else would they be there without a warrant, without a cause?

A trusted insider from the city frantically called my mom and informed her that the police officers were there to keep an eye on Daddy. They were looking for any chance to arrest him and take him to the police station. I couldn't believe it. Were the police officers really there to invent a reason to arrest him? Were those who are supposed to protect really plotting to harm? Really? Seriously!?

My mother, rushed to the office, heart pounding and eyes ablaze. She was on the verge of what seemed like a breakdown as she fiercely and passionately wanted to safeguard her husband. Maa is one powerhouse of incomprehensible energy! She was a lioness refusing to see her mate torn apart.

"Have you people completely lost your humanity!" she cried out when she got to the office. "If you take him, you take me as well take me too. Karo arrest! Innocent logon ko, karo harass! Is this what the police is for?"

Her voice cracked the air like thunder. Cameras were rolling. Reporters circled. This was footage they did not want to miss. The media people were capturing all this craziness on camera, as Maa went on. "I'm telling you," she yelled, "my husband is God's anointed man! If you touch him, God's wrath will fall on you and your families."

We were trying to calm her down, to quiet her eruption. "Maa, it's okay, Maa. Let's go home. Daddy will be okay." But she was unstoppable.

When the police officers saw that their misdeeds were on display for everyone to see and this spectacle was being caught on multiple cameras, they reluctantly agreed to let us go home. They too were shaken. Everyone was. But even as we left, the officers surrounded us and made us feel like criminals, as though the courts had declared us guilty.

There was one police vehicle in front of us and another behind us. The crowds around the building followed us – mostly people from the city and the church to show their support. We felt surrounded by love, prayers, and solidarity from people from every walk of life.

I called Lee who was at home with our son. "Please don't allow Baaba to come out of the house. I don't want him to see this drama. It is pretty crazy out here. It's a circus. Please just stay inside."

Lee had just returned from attending his brother's engagement celebration in Napa Valley and now, more than ever, my husband just wanted to safely take us back home, not to Damoh but to the home we had built together by the alpine beauty.

The number of police officers kept on increasing. My mother stood her ground. She had to tell them that they were unwelcome on our campus and that they dare not keep the supportive crowds locked outside the gates.

The crowds that were standing in support came inside the gates.

We were so humbled to see people pouring out their tears and beautiful prayers. Every time I think of it, I salute their courage. They stood for hours, weeping and praying

US Citizens Unlawfully Detained

knees to the ground and hands to the heavens. Even now, I carry their courage like a salve.

In the US, the word *fascism* gets thrown around too easily. Having lived through the persecution and threats and experienced the fear in every corner of life, I no longer say that fascism is on the rise in America. Far from it!

I have lived under its shadow, and now I know what real fascism is.

In the United States, people still speak up. Loudly. Every day one can tune into shows like *The View*, where powerful, intelligent women openly present their thoughts. They challenge presidents, debate policy, and call out injustice without fear holding them back. Protests happen in broad daylight. That is democracy.

In India, things are different. Far different.

There, people are terrified to speak, to post, to even like a social media comment that questions the ruling ideology of Hindu nationalism and extremism. People whisper, glance over their shoulders, and fall silent when the topic turns to religious minorities or dissent.

Forget calling out those in power by name; most people are too afraid to stand alongside someone who's already being targeted. The fear isn't abstract. It is visceral. And it is everywhere.

After living under that kind of shadow, I see the difference. And yet, in the midst of that environment people stood with us for hours and hours crying, praying, and fighting. They knew that righteousness does not promise safety, but it does require resilience.

My parents carried that resilience in their bones. They didn't retaliate. They didn't accuse. They simply stood firm, rooted in their faith. They faced down the forces of hatred and fear, not with violence or retaliation but with the quiet strength of those who know they are fighting for something greater than themselves. Their children and grandchildren got to witness their unwavering commitment to truth, even when the truth is inconvenient, even when its cost feels heavy-laden.

God was watching. And people remember. This was the talk of the town.

And then something unexpected happened.

Many of the police officers who were surrounding our home where people whose lives had been impacted by what my parents and grandparents had built. Someone from their family had been educated at a Christian school. Someone had been treated at the mission hospital for free. Someone had their own life spared because the hospital never ran out of oxygen during the pandemic. One officer was in tears because he remembered how when his family ran out of groceries, my grandmother quietly sent them two weeks' worth of food. But now, they were forced to fulfill their duties so they could continue feeding their families.

My dad with his oh so very tender Indian heart ordered chai and samosas and then dinner for all the police officers.

"What the heck, Daddy!" I said, feeling exhausted and disgusted by the drama and the trauma of the day.

"Well, when someone comes to our home, we offer them hospitality. It doesn't matter who they are."

I rolled my eyes. "Okay, whatever. Please get some sleep."

Then I went to check on my son and make sure he went to bed on time. I knew this town was no longer safe. My husband felt strongly too that Damoh was no longer a safe place for us. Despite the victories in the courts and sympathy from the people, the mob mentality of the goons had influenced the police, and we had experienced a glimpse of what happens when there is a collusion of influential figures and misconduct by the local authorities. The collusion was undeniable, or perhaps the authorities were the ones acting as the goons.

We decided to leave that night with our son, Maa, my brother, and sister-in-law. They had nothing against us. We had nothing to hide. We packed two cars in full view of the officers that were there. Lee, Baba, and I were in one car, and the rest of the group were in the car ahead of us. No one stopped us as we drove out of the campus. Why would they?

# 12

Vigilant and on Edge

My father was not apprehended that night, but the dread of that taking place loomed over us. We drove from the residential campus and were trying to get to a safe place, were we could freely breathe and travel to the next destination. A police officer with haughty eyes and the ugliest moustache pulled his car in front of ours to stop us.

"They are stopping us, but you guys please go ahead." I called my brother.

"No, we'll be right there. Don't worry. We'll face this together, Didi." My brother tried to find words to comfort. They drove back to be with us.

Our cars had been stopped in the middle of Marutal village. The air was filled with familiar smells of the earth, wood, and smoke, the darkness punctuated by the eerie glow of torches and the murmurs of a growing crowd. Special forces had been sent to our home by the state. And for what? To illegally detain my family. Four out of the six of us were U.S. citizens. The police officers swarmed again, without a warrant. Hours of agony and confusion!

Reporters hovered like vultures, their cameras ready to capture our disgrace, while the police—two hundred strong now—milled about like a pack of wolves waiting for the signal to strike. Yet among them were some who stood tall, their pens, cameras, and duties wielded not as weapons, but as instruments of truth. The honorable journalists, officers, and people of Damoh, bore witness to our rawness with integrity. Their questions were thoughtful, their presence a quiet testament to the belief that even in our most fragile moments, there was dignity worth preserving.

The resilience of our people surrounded us with strength and prayers to combat the night's heavy darkness. But not all came in service of truth. Some who hovered were there to frame our suffering as a headline designed to sell. Whatever they captured—whether with grace or greed—was released to the world. It went viral. Our vulnerability, our plight, was laid bare for all to see.

And yet, as those images spread like wildfire, thousands dropped to their knees in places far and near, hands clasped in prayer for people they may never meet. Strangers wept for us. They felt the hollow ache of losing a place called home, of being stripped from the land that cradled the bones of our ancestors. They understood, in some quiet place within themselves, the pain of belonging torn away.

Inside the car, these prayers helped me stay calm so as not to frighten my twelve-year-old son, any more than he already was. He stayed strong. My husband was sitting in the front seat.

He turned around and asked our son, "You doing okay, buddy?"

Our son, trying to keep humor alive, said, "Daddy, if they try to open my door, I'm ready to pull a Mike Tyson one-two on them."

We were exhausted and our perseverance was being tested. I rolled my window down, desperate for a crack of reason in the madness. A female officer passed by, her uniform stiff, her expression harder. I caught her eye.

"There's a kid in this car," I said, forcing assertiveness in my voice. "You're probably a mother, right? You know children shouldn't be a part of all this."

My words, meant to stir her humanity, were met by coldness. She smirked. She spit out her words like they were cheap, mocking me with the sarcastic use of the word *friend*:

"Oye, yaar. Kitna bolti hai."

I wasn't her *yaar*.

"Watch your tone when you talk to me," I said, each syllable sharp as broken glass.

Suddenly, a shout pierced the night.

It was the voice of my mother, pleading with an officer who stood, chest puffed, his ugly moustache twitching, like some absurd caricature of authority.

"Your husband is the accused criminal!" the man bellowed, his ugly beer belly shaking as though his cruelty had given him power.

In his face I saw every insecure man who had ever tried to use his uniform to compensate for his own smallness. Ramesh, our driver, folded his hands in front of me. "Didi, please don't get out of the car. I beg you," he whispered, the lines on his face deep with worry.

But I couldn't sit still. I didn't know I had the capacity to feel this level of disgust as I felt for this man who was rudely speaking to my mother. The injustice was too loud. I swung open the door, feet hitting the dust like a challenge. "How dare you call my father a criminal," I shouted. "When he has given fifty years to this community! You—who will be forgotten—dare to tarnish his name because of his faith! Because he's a Christian leader!" I pointed at the officer's face, shaking with the force of my own fury. "This is harassment! Illegal, immoral harassment! The world will know what you're doing here in Damoh!"

Some reporters captured that moment and the video went viral.

"Didi, please," came the urgent whispers from the people around me, tugging at my arms. "Get back in the car."

I did. But not because I was afraid. No, fear had long left me. I did it because they needed to know we won't suffer quietly.

The police, for all their posturing, must've known we were on the edge of something. They finally agreed to let us stay detained in our cars just a minute away from my father's office campus. Still detained. Still under their watchful, leering eyes. There were six of us in those cars. Four were US citizens.

We contacted the consulate in Mumbai and reported the incident to the State Department. My husband contacted our lawyer in the States, and she was sharp as steel, pressing the police with questions.

They lied, of course. "They are not being detained," they said. But Lee had the videos, each second of their deceit.

After being detained for hours, the superintendent of police finally showed up around 2:00 a.m., but he couldn't meet my gaze. I'd met him once before, just days earlier in his office. I'd asked him humbly to stop this harassment. He'd sat there feigning sympathy. But now, in the dead of night, his mask had slipped. He knew I saw through him. Standing there, his silence screamed his guilt.

"This is wrong," I told him, my voice low but cutting. "And you know it. You can stop this; you should stop this. Do something good with the power you have."

Like a lifeless idol, he said nothing. Just climbed into his vehicle and drove off to our house where he would break in and vandalize it. His team shattered the windows, chipped off the wood, overturned and broke the furniture. They ransacked the place. The ate our food, stole our books and laptops, and then return them later like petty thieves ashamed of their own actions. The week before, mobs had been hired to burn effigies of my dad, but none of those men were arrested. I wanted to know why, and this man had no answers.

Reporters circled our cars. My brother spoke first. His voice was steady even under the weight of all that had happened. "This harassment. They are trying so hard to destroy us, mentally and emotionally," he said.

My brother talked about how the police forced themselves into my dad's office without a warrant. They were trying to intimidate us by asking questions that we had already answered in the seemingly countless inquires that had been conducted on my dad's institution between 2022 and 2024. They were questioning things that had been cleared by the High Court. The men harassing my father acted like slaves to the goons who had pressured them to do this instead of actually protecting the country and its upstanding citizens. I told them as much.

"Everything is happening in front of everyone to see. Everyone can see who is being constructive and who is being destructive. Who has worked to benefit education, healthcare, employment when people needed it the most?"

These viral videos brought more people to pray for us, and we will be forever grateful for those prayers!

I told the reporters what Daddy had always said to us. "The people of Damoh are our people," I told them. "No matter where I die, this is where I want to be buried—the place where seven generations of our family members have been buried."

Perhaps an overtrained and overstrained mind doesn't hold the capacity to comprehend that kind of devotion. That type of attachment never made sense to me. Who cares where I am buried once I'm dead? The connection and the emotion that Daddy felt with this place was something I never understood. Now, more than ever, it didn't make any sense. But at that moment we were in a position where we had to put emotions aside and just take the next practical steps that we needed to take.

It is healthy to break off an abusive relationship. Enough is enough!

We had always been there, always worked in the midst of the people as though we were one big family. And now, this!

"Where is your father?" they asked. "We heard he's not at home."

Did they really expect me to answer that question? The last time I saw him, he was there at home, surrounded by two hundred officers. Shouldn't they know? Shouldn't they be keeping track? But there was a sinking pit in my stomach, and I prayed, silently and desperately for his safety. At 6:30 a.m., with dawn bleeding into the sky, I made one last call to Jayant Malaya, a BJP leader but an old friend of my grandfather's. I hoped he could still see beyond the politics. As always, he answered like a true gentleman. "My twelve-year-old son slept in a car surrounded by these people," I said, my voice cracking. "This isn't legal. This isn't right. Please, your word carries weight."

Even though hesitant at first, to his credit, he made the call. And by 6:40 a.m., the nightmare seemed to come to a halt.

We were told we could leave. But the damage had been done. The wound between us and the place we had always called home was now deep and festering. It is what it is. A wound. And, in time, wounds heal.

13

Abrupt Transitions

The local police had vandalized my parents' home in Damoh, trashing it in an effort to intimidate us. They detained us unlawfully, filed false accusations against my loved ones, and allowed mobs to burn effigies of my father in the streets, yet no arrests were made. Through it all, we refused to be silenced. This wasn't just religious persecution; it was a systematic attempt to destroy anyone who dared challenge the prevailing narrative of hatred and exclusion. This wasn't just a matter of religious freedom; this was a gross violation of fundamental human rights!

Leaders from all walks of life—the friends who showed up at our doorstep, the strangers who sent us messages of support—they were all part of this struggle. They reminded us that while the storm may have been fierce, it had not succeeded in breaking us. And more importantly, it had not succeeded in silencing us.

It had been one of the strangest weeks of my life. In the midst of this storm, we stood with our arms lifted in prayer, knowing that our hope is not in worldly power but in the light of Christ, which cannot be extinguished.

The police detained us till 6:40 a.m. and we were on our way to the nearest airport which was two hours away. Early that morning, my daughter received a message from us. "Daddy is on his way to pick you up from school. We'll be leaving for America tomorrow evening."

Everyone at her school was in shock when she shared with them the news of the abrupt transitions our family was facing. They surrounded her with prayers, love, tears, and heartfelt good wishes. Our baby girl had to keep her tender heart strong. She cared so deeply and loved so passionately.

Lee went from the drama we had endured the night before to a two-hour drive to the Jabalpur airport from Damoh to catch a flight to Hyderabad and then another one to Coimbatore. Then he had a four-hour taxi ride to the boarding school. He helped our baby girl wrap up this chapter of her life. She had so many questions and wanted to know all the details of who, what, when, where, and why behind everything that had happened with our family. We were all sleep deprived and just wanting everyone to be safe. Baba and I met up with them in Delhi.

Since our house in Damoh had been vandalized by the police, we couldn't return to Damoh to pack our suitcases. Some of the staff packed our suitcases for us and met up with us in Delhi where I went through everything and packed and unpacked whatever we needed to before we were finally on our way back to America.

We were advised not to use our phones, so we didn't get to see anyone or say goodbye or have any way to fully know that our loved ones are safe. It was all very odd and

Abrupt Transitions

abrupt, heavy like a nightmare I wish I could have wakened from. But we were fine. At least our children were safely away from a culture that teaches people to judge others based on their caste and religious labels.

I left with some peace knowing that at the Supreme Court, Mr. Kapil Sibal, known for his integrity, was working on Daddy's case meticulously, leaving no stone unturned because he knew that our life, liberty, and rights were being violated by powerful adversaries. He was willing to take on Daddy's case pro bono. Then there was another person who was constantly there with his unwavering support, Senior advocate, Mr. Vivek Tankha, a Kashmiri Brahmin who carries a powerful celestial aura and who speaks with conviction, every word carefully chosen to reflect the truth of our circumstances. At the district level, advocate Anunay Shrivastava, was honoring his father's legacy and was unafraid to stand alone with his commitment to truth no matter how difficult the fight.

Because I knew that there were people of integrity protecting my loved ones, I was able to leave with a less heavy heart as I walked through the Delhi airport.

We had not slept that week. But even in the chaos, God was still at work. We had won another court case. The Jabalpur High Court ruled that the charges against my father were baseless. The judge saw through the malicious claims and dismissed the charges. The judge even stated that the local authorities had misused their positions of authority to defame my father. It was a collective victory for all who stood by us, but there were more battles to come. Advocate Shashank Shekhar was fighting on our behalf. He never treated us as just clients but as people, as family, whose lives he was striving to protect.

On August 31, 2024, two weeks after I returned to America, , the local media in Damoh spread another false rumor, claiming my father had fled the country. The same superintendent of police who vandalized our home, placed international travel restrictions on my father and brother, and detained us unlawfully, Mr. Shruitkriti Somwanshi, gave the statement to the local media: "Not sure how he escaped. Maybe though Nepal or somewhere else. But we'll find out."

Just like previous times when the local media had called my dad and Uncle Dave a *chor* (Hindi for thief) just to create and uproar and to vilify them in public, this time Mr. Somwanshi, the superintendent of police in Damoh, joined in that sick chorus to tarnish my father's reputation. But our senior lawyer and honorable Member of Parliament, Mr. Vivek Tankha, released a video on Twitter of my father standing beside him at his office in Delhi, refuting the lies. Even as we waited for the travel restrictions to lift, we held onto hope, trusting that God was still working through it all.

The prayers of people who cared became our lifeline. Three weeks passed, and finally, on September 23, my sister's birthday, we received the news we had prayed for—the High Court declared all charges null and void. The court recognized that the allegations were driven by malice, designed to tarnish Daddy's reputation and to stop the good work that was going on. The system had tried to silence justice, but righteousness prevailed.

Abrupt Transitions

God allowed us to witness significant victories in a legal battles. This was a victory, but we needed to see an end to the unnecessary yet ongoing battles.

Perhaps the tide was turning after all. We could only hope.

My parents, brother, and sister-in-law remained in India, still facing the weight of unjust persecution. God was doing something in the background that we didn't fully comprehend.

14

Freedom Unfolding

In the tired eyes of my family, I saw not just fatigue but something far deeper, an ache tempered by resolve. Uncle Dave's body was frail, but his presence remained unwavering. Aunt Sheeja was like a weathered tree that has learned to bend with the storm but refuses to fall. Daddy and Maa, though battered by public scorn and private betrayals, carried with them a quiet certainty: That justice delayed is not justice denied. That God, though sometimes silent in the chaos, was not absent.

As for me, my husband, and children, leaving India was bittersweet. There were no screams when we left, only the sound of rolling suitcases, hurried prayers, and the hum of fluorescent lights overhead in the New Delhi airport—cold and indifferent to the devastation they illuminated. As I clutched my children's hands, my husband just steps ahead, I turned for one last look, not at a city or terminal gate but something intangible, a life, a sense of belonging that was being stripped away.

This was not just some struggle for name or faith or land. It was a battle for the soul of a community. It mirrored a larger shift across nations and boarders where truth was being traded for propaganda. The question was not whether we would survive this particular storm. The question was what kind of people we would be on the other side of it. Would we allow the betrayals and the violence to harden our hearts, or would we rise above them, clinging to the values that had always defined us?

I sobbed as I walked through immigration. What a week it had been! Even as the flight lifted into the night sky, I kept praying, not for escape but for protection. For those we had left behind. For the house and the trees and the gardens. For my family that had been marked as criminals for no crime but caring too loudly, too faithfully, too openly.

Yet, in every place where power tried to silence people, there remained those who resisted. Judges who clung to conscience. Lawyers who braved intimidation. Ordinary people who dared to speak when it would have been easier to disappear. These, I believe, are the quiet revolutionaries of our time, not because they stormed the gates, but because they stand firm when the walls tremble.

To keep my sanity, I had to surrender to the quiet moments of reflection in the memories of those who had gone before us. My grandfather Vj had built this family not on wealth or status but on service. He lived through famines, wars, political upheavals, yet never once did he seek to hoard power. His strength was not in dominance but in nurturing. In his hands, leadership looked like care. Dada's memory whispers to me even now: *Do not mistake silence for surrender, nor gentleness for weakness.*

That legacy, once passed down in stories over chai and soil-stained mornings in the garden, now lived in our struggle. And in that struggle, I saw a lineage of strength, an inheritance no title deed could contain. Our community, bruised but unbroken, surrounded us with prayers, hands, presence.

In the days that followed, we needed to rebuild physically, mentally, emotionally, and spiritually. Rebuilding came in waves. Some days were steady; others were steeped in grief. It was not just our home in Damoh that had been vandalized by the police. It was not just a place that needed repair, but also our sense of safety, of meaning, of trust. But even in the rubble, there were glimmers of hope. A child's laughter. A stranger's kindness. The persistence of memory. These small moments became sacraments, reminders that healing is slow but sacred.

We had come back to America, not as strangers but as returning daughters and sons. This land had always been home too, not just by birth but by breath. The Rockies stood as they always had—majestic, silent, unmoved by the chaos we had left behind. Their ridges, carved by time and weather, mirrored the new contours forming in my soul. In their quiet strength, I found a peace that had always felt more like my own skin.

Still, something inside us remained suspended. We hadn't gone to India for adventure. We had returned to a legacy. My parents had held on to the house, the garden, the land of our foremothers and forefathers, not out of nostalgia but reverence. It was treated like sacred ground, stitched with sacrifice and service. And so we had gone back. Not just to honor that history but to live inside it for a while. We had returned because of love.

But now, we were here again—and they were still there. My parents. Our loved ones. I wanted them with me. I wanted the whole family to be here beneath the endless skies of alpine majesty. I wanted the freedom and peace I felt in the shadow of the Rockies to wrap around them too. Not just safety but stillness. Not just survival but belonging.

There were days when despair knocked loudly. When the headlines spun falsehoods, and the betrayers walked free. In those moments, I would return to stillness, not the silence of retreat but the stillness of surrender. The kind of surrender that Mosses spoke of: "The Lord will fight for you; you need only to be still" (Exodus 14:14).

In returning to that stillness, something began to stir. A deeper knowing. A sharper clarity. In moments of deep injustice, faith is not a passive thing. It is an uprising of the soul. To believe that God is fighting alongside us—even through us—is to life with courage in a world that demands compliance. I realized that the battle we were living through was not just ours. It echoed through time and across borders. What we experienced was part of a larger unravelling: the spread of fear masquerading as patriotism, or violence cloaked in religiosity, or control sold as peace. History was groaning under the weight of old wounds being reopened, and new ones carved with frightening precision.

The storm had not destroyed us. It had revealed us.

In times of crisis, the truth has a way of surfacing. The chaos caused by those with fascist tendencies forced us to confront uncomfortable truths about people we considered our own. We had to choose between passive acceptance and active resistance. It's tempting to believe that being peaceful, being passive, is the Christlike way to respond. But too often, that's just an excuse to hide one's own insecurities, a defense mechanism against the feeling of helplessness. Yes, God fights on our behalf, but he also works through people like my father and mother—people who refuse to back down, who courageously stand on the frontlines when the battle demands it.

As the days unfolded, we began to rebuild, not just across borders but within ourselves. We rebuilt through early morning prayers. Through late-night conversations where the trauma cracked open and the light slowly bled in. We rebuilt by naming our pain without shame. We rebuilt by refusing to let bitterness take root.

What became clearer in the aftermath of the storm was not just who harmed us but who remained silent. Silence is rarely neutral. Too often, it is the mask that fear wears while pretending to be polite. The quiet indifference of those who looked away when my father's name was being slandered. The way some leaders—men who once preached about justice—turned their backs when it came with a cost. Their silence was louder than any accusation.

And yet this too became a revelation: fascism does not rise only through brute force. It rises through the soft complicity of those who value comfort over conscience. Through small betrayals—a missed signature, a hushed conversation, a refusal to speak up or show up—until the structure of integrity begins to crumble.

In exile, you begin to see more clearly: who showed up and who stayed silent. Whose allegiance was to truth and whose was to comfort. Fascism does not flourish because of strong men alone; it grows in the soil of silence, of people who choose personal peace over prophetic courage.

And yet even as we mourned the betrayals—of leaders who should have spoken and did not, of kin who turned away—we also bore witnesses to a different kind of miracle. Strangers knelt in prayer across continents. Journalists risked backlash to report the truth. Ordinary people—teachers, priests, students—stood up when those in power shrank back. It was as though in the face of cruelty something ancient had been awakened. A deeper call. A fiercer love.

And now I understand that the true battle is not for dominance; it is for dignity. For the ability to love with one's head high and soul intact. For those of my dear loved ones who are reevaluating their sense of home and identity and belonging, I so want them to revel in the fact that ironically exile feels like an invitation—to deeper faith, to a wider vision, to radical trust.

While the trauma of that time still clings like smoke so does grace. The people who linked arms with us. The unexpected kindness and courage. The resilience of children who adapt to abrupt transitions before adults even find their footing. My son was just twelve when he cracked jokes in the face of a police raid. My daughter, who packed up her home away from home in boarding school within hours of notice, whispered a prayer, "God please protect Meemaw and Papa." My husband kept on reassuring me of truth's stubbornness in the midst of it all.

Like the roots of the imili tree, truth holds on even when the winds rage. And when the dust finally settles, the question remains: Who stood firm? Who watered the roots when they chopped off the tree? Those gardens may be far away, but their seeds live in our witness.

Our home was ransacked. My father's name dragged through mud. But deeper still ran the calling—to remember who we are and what we are here to become. Not victims of violence but victors of truth. Not bitter but brave. Not hardened but holy.

The storm exposed many things—the cowardice of those we once trusted, the greed of those who sold their soul for momentary solace. But it also revealed the fierce resilience of love, the power of prayer, and the sacred defiance of standing your ground even when the earth shakes beneath you.

So here we are. We get to rebuild not just walls and windows but faith. Not just reputations but resolve. Not just a home of bricks but of belonging. A faith not built on fear but on freedom. A future not forged by hate but by healing.

15

Reflections In Flight

We didn't just leave India; we were pulled away from it not with ceremony or closure but with urgency. No time for long hugs or thoughtful goodbyes. Just quiet nods, tense shoulders, the sound of wheels on concrete, and a heaviness that settled over everything like dust. We boarded the flight with one foot still stuck in the soil of this motherland and the other already stepping into a life that was waiting for us back in the Rockies.

We left from Delhi. This city will always be a very special place for our family. This was the place where my husband and I got married. It was a place to escape from the small-town intensity of Damoh for delicious food and bookstores. It was always a joy to shop there. We breathed deeper and laughed a little louder when there. But this time, there was no laughter. Just the surreal calm of an airport that moved too fast.

My parents were still there. Their safety was uncertain. Their movements were restricted by orders from people who had never cared to understand who they were or what they stood for. We were leaving, and they were staying.

That was the sentence playing over and over in my mind. I so desperately wished we were all leaving together.

As the plane lifted off, I looked out over the sprawling lights of a city that had never been home but which, for a moment, held everything we loved. As the lights disappeared into the haze, I closed my eyes and let the silence stretch for a long moment.

There had been no map for this kind of transition. The children sensed the weight of it all, even if they didn't have the words yet. India for them had always been a kind of wonderland: the stories, the family, the colors, the flavors. And yet something had changed. They saw how easily love could be turned into suspicion. How quickly kindness could be framed as threat. And how even the sacred could be twisted to justify fear.

Our daughter had to leave her boarding school with barely a moment's notice. It was a place she loved deeply with its mist-shrouded peaks, dorm parents who cheered her on, and friends who were starting to feel like siblings. She had found her rhythm there. And yet when we told her it was time to go, she understood.

The farewell was short but beautiful. Her friends and dorm parents gathered around her with misty eyes. There was a cake on the table and love in every word. It wasn't extravagant, but it was enough. It was the kind of goodbye that says you are seen. You are loved. Go in peace.

She carried both ache and anticipation in equal measure, with grace. In that way, she mirrored all of us.

We were returning to a place we knew well. A place where the streets were familiar, the air clearer, the rules predictable. We were headed back to a life shaped by privilege, a life of comforts: good schools, protected rights, and a system that still offered a far greater sense of order than the chaos we had just witnessed.

There was relief in that. But it wasn't euphoric. It was layered.

In India, we had learned something deeper about community. About the slow, patient work of service. About what it means to plant roots in places that the world overlooks. And walking away from that—no matter how justified—still carried weight.

Somewhere over the North Atlantic I remembered a line that had once stayed with me like a stone in my pocket. David Livermore wrote:

> Jesus seems to say, "I represent and embody a different kind of kingdom. My kingdom is one where the underdog wins. Mine is one where we subversively overthrow existing kingdoms by turning the other cheek… It looks different from any earthly kingdom you've ever experienced."

That line landed differently now. It wasn't just a theological idea. It was the reality we had lived. Our family offered dignity, healthcare, education, a place of healing. And in return, we were treated as threats by those who clung to a version of India too small to hold people like us.

Daddy had always believed that love must speak louder than fear. Even when mobs gathered and our family was targeted he kept showing up to work. Kept treating people with compassion. Kept believing that there was still hope for the land that raised him. It remained a mission aligned with a higher kingdom—a kingdom that defied earthly power structures, one that refused to succumb to hatred or retaliation.

I thought of the little girl from the village who was diagnosed with a rare blood disorder. Her family couldn't afford the costly bone marrow transplant that would save her life. But someone cared enough. Arrangements were made. A premier healthcare institution in Vellore accepted her case. These Christian leaders who cared did not ask for anything in return. No conversion demands. Just care. Just kindness.

That kindness was twisted into suspicion by those in power. As if healing a child could be a crime. The anti-conversion laws weren't protecting anyone. They were punishing people for believing differently. For loving differently. For living in ways that didn't conform to the dominant script.

But we weren't alone. All over the country, people like us—quiet workers, bridge-builders, believers in a bigger story—were being watched, targeted, discredited. The strategy was clear: intimidate and isolate.

Even WhatsApp, the most widely used messaging platform in the country, had threatened to pull out over new surveillance rules. It wasn't just about an app. It was about control. About monitoring dissent. About labelling any alternative vision as dangerous.

And yet, even with all that pressure, we hadn't left in shame. We had left in truth.

Reflections In Flight

Our family's legacy in Damoh was not one of silence or surrender. It was rooted In generations who had poured their lives into that soil through medicine, education, advocacy, and care. During the pandemic, our hospital had saved hundreds. We were the only facility in the region with an operational oxygen plant. Our cardiac care, dialysis, and outreach programs kept people alive in a time when the government was overwhelmed.

People told us, "If you leave, the town will lose its heart."

But we knew something deeper: the work was never ours alone. It was bigger than us. It was God's work, and it would continue with or without us. The people will remember the faith in Christ that compelled us to do good anyways. Once we get out of the way, hopefully Christ's greatness will be realized more potently.

When we landed in America, it felt different than before. Not just a return but a reckoning.

The sky over the Rockies stretched wide and open. The air smelled of pine. There were no layers of dust. No watchful eyes. The pace slowed. The silence felt full. And that first week, rainbows arched across the sky—again and again. Double arcs of color bending over us like promises we didn't even know how to ask for. This wasn't the end of the story. It was the beginning of a new one.

Our house welcomed us with warmth and routine. The children started school the very next morning. Backpacks slung over tired shoulders, the comfort of classroom rituals eased the chaos of the previous days. There was no time to process. Just movement. But even in that movement, healing began.

This was a place where we could be fully ourselves. We could rest without looking over our shoulders. We could live out our faith without accusation. We could parent without fear.

As I unpacked our bags and put fresh sheets on the beds, part of me remained stretched across the ocean still listening for news from Damoh, still holding space for my parents, still wondering how long until we could be together again. I longed for them to be here. To taste the stillness of these mountains. To know this quiet. To be free to walk under the same wide skies. Not to be just safe but restored.

A home isn't just a house. It's people. It's the ability to exhale.

And I wanted that for all of us.

The days passed. Slowly, rhythm returned. The kids found their laughter again. We began to cook, to talk, to dream aloud. The care from our loved ones here helped us cling to faith when fear could have easily taken over even as we held onto the reminder of what we left and why it mattered.

And so we keep going. Still holding onto the stories. Still building from the ground up. Still believing in that other kingdom, the one where the underdog wins. The one that doesn't bow to fear. The one that lifts from below, that heals with gentleness, that quietly refuses to be crushed.

We were not broken. We were becoming. There would be greater hope of restoration in the days ahead.

For those moments, in the shadow of the Rockies, that felt like enough.

16

The Stillness That Speaks

There's a kind of stillness in the Rockies that made me want to believe again. I didn't have certainty or the answers, but there was a presence. There was something deeper, older, wiser in the mountains, like they know something they're not yet willing to share.

Some mornings I step outside with a cup of coffee and let the chill wrap around me like a shawl. The sky stretches endlessly above. The deer graze in the park outside our home without a care in the world. Pine needles glisten in the light. It's hard to hold onto bitterness when the world feels this open.

And yet, tucked beneath the surface of this silence is a story. Our story. One that carried us across oceans, through upheaval, through fire. The dust of Damoh still clings to us . . . sometimes, even here among the clean lines of mountain ridges. We may have left the noise, the threats, the constant fear, but we are still letting go of the ache. That kind of ache takes time to heal, but it will never remain a part of us.

Here in this silence, I've begun to understand peace in a way I never could before.

It's what the spiritual leader Father Richard Rohr calls the path of descent—the wisdom that only comes when you stop resisting the dark and instead, let it teach you how to see. "The journey to the true self," he writes, "always passes through the shadowlands."

I'm still trying to understand that, even though we have passed through the shadowlands.

And we are still standing.

I think about the India I grew up loving—the kaleidoscope of festivals, the heat rising from clay rooftops, the call of church bells and the call to prayer echoing over narrow streets, and the people singing their scriptures on temple loudspeakers. It was a place that held contradiction and communion in the same breath.

But something has shifted.

And we are not supposed to talk about it.

We are supposed to clap when the lights come on at political rallies. Are we supposed to cheer for economic progress while children in tribal schools drink from dried-up wells? Are we supposed to say that faith is thriving even as churches are burned and pastors are beaten?

Are we supposed to forget the families in Manipur living in relief tents? Are we to ignore the people lynched on suspicion because they look different from the majority? Are we to overlook the laws that are designed to erase not to protect?

We are told it's about culture.

About unity.

About pride. But pride that demands silence is not patriotism. And fear when mixed with religiosity becomes a deadly thing. I have no problem with faith. I have a problem with its performance. Religiosity when untethered from love becomes a costume. A kind of moral theater where the rituals are right, but the heart is missing. This isn't new.

My Jewish grandmother told stories of indulgences being sold like tickets to heaven. My Middle Eastern great-grandfather, with his Islamic roots, had stories of a faith that was whispered in secret because it was safer that way. In both stories, I heard the same thing: the divine distorted.

And now, in India, I see the same story wearing new clothes. Hindutva is not Hinduism. Hinduism is vast, philosophical, gentle, mystical. Hindutva is not. It is a political machine. And like all ideologies that seek power, it must first find an enemy. It has chosen Muslims. It has chosen Christians.

It has chosen anyone who dares to speak, to serve, to stand outside the lines.

My family, was not unique. But we were visible. And visibility can be dangerous in a world where the truth is a threat.

I think about the children who watched their churches burn in Manipur. I think about my own children, who once thought of India as a place just shy of heaven, now asking questions I never wanted them to ask. I think about the pastors who pray with one eye open and the women who still light candles in bombed-out churches. And I think of my father. His quiet strength. His unwavering faith. His belief that love would win. That light did not need to scream to be heard. That is the kingdom I believe in. The one David Livermore described: "A kingdom where the underdog wins... where justice is not just a fleeting victory but a reflection of something eternal." It's not the kingdom of grand gestures and empty rituals. It's the one built through daily faithfulness. Through healing the sick. Teaching the child. Standing with the forgotten. That's the kingdom I want to hand down.

Sometimes, when the wind brushes through the pines just right, I think of Dada and Dadi's garden. Of the tamarind trees, tall and knotted, holding the scent of stories. Of how we'd gather their fruit in baskets, sticky fingers and sour-sweet mouths, the sun slanting just so. Of how those trees knew us. Held us. Watched us become. Those trees didn't ask for attention. They stood. They stayed. Their roots ran deep not because they were untouched by storms but because they had learned how to bend. I want to be like that. And I want my children to carry that same rootedness. Not in nationalism or fear but in something truer. I want them to plant new trees in the soil of these mountains, knowing they are still connected to the ones that came before.

The Rockies don't hold my ancestors. But they hold my prayers. They are our new home—because they are where we are learning to begin again.

To listen.
To breathe.
To become.

I want to teach my children that justice and mercy are not political positions. They are spiritual postures that come out of walking humbly with our God. That every faith tradition has a story of the poor, the overlooked, the exiled—and that's not a coincidence. That's the invitation. Because the world doesn't need more religiosity. It needs more rootedness. More love that lasts longer than the headlines. So what do we do?

We unmask. We tell the truth. We teach our children to do the same. To plant with open hands. To build community across borders, belief systems, and bruises.

We stop letting rituals replace relationship. We stop worshipping flags more than we love people. We stop confusing control with holiness. We resist what dehumanizes. We reclaim faith as a river not a wall.

I hope one day my grandchildren will sit with me here beneath this sky, and I will be able to tell them about tamarind trees and exile and love that refused to die. I will tell them about how faith is not what kept us from suffering but what carried us through it.

And when they ask what it means to follow the path of Jesus, I'll tell them: It means holding onto hope when the headlines say otherwise. It means loving louder than the hate. It means rooting deep—even in foreign soil—because you know who you are. It means never mistaking religion for God.

And if I've done that well—if we've done that well—maybe they will carry the story forward.

Maybe they'll plant their own trees.

17

When Mountains Move

"The hills are alive with the sound of music." Ah, that timeless melody once echoed through our living room like a benediction. *The Sound of Music* wasn't just a film; it was a family favorite. The story where resilience triumphed, beauty endured, and goodness prevailed. A story we turned to for comfort, for inspiration, for joy.

But now, I can't bring myself to watch it. The parallels feel too raw.

Captain von Trapp's quiet grief as he watches his beloved Austria fall to authoritarian rule. His inner turmoil as he's asked to betray his conscience. His family's breathless escape into the mountains—not for adventure but for survival. It all hits a bit too close to home.

We didn't climb over the Alps. We flew over oceans. We didn't hide in convents. We moved through airports, praying for safe passage. But the ache? The ache was the same.

I was so incredibly thankful when my parents and the rest of the family finally arrived safely to the United States.

They didn't leave because we stopped loving India. They left because India stopped protecting those who loved her most.

I think often about Captain von Trapp who once sang for his country but could no longer sing with it. That story used to feel like history, and now it feels like us. I remember watching the von Trapp children sing together with their father—their voices gentle, trembling with hope. I remember how their music became a quiet act of defiance.

When the shift in India was taking place, at some point, people stopped asking questions and started following orders. "Working under pressure," I've heard those officers say one too many times.

Now as a family and as individuals, we are trying to find our rhythm and melody and how it all works out together. The soil that once felt like home suddenly cracked beneath us. Like Austria, toward the end of the film, the India we knew and cherished is changing. The air has shifted.

There was a time when to be Christian in India meant being known as someone who served quietly and faithfully in hospitals, schools, and orphanages. It meant love in action not power in politics. But now, even compassion is seen as conversion. Even service is viewed as subversion.

Religious persecution is no longer a distant whisper; it's a weight pressing heavily.

And like the von Trapps, we are forced to ask: What must we leave behind in order to protect what we love?

This new version of India did not rise overnight.

It was built, brick by brick, on silence.

In 2002, the world watched as Gujarat erupted in fire and blood.

More than a thousand people, mostly Muslims, were killed. The images were unforgettable: homes burned, women brutalized, children orphaned. Modi, then chief minister, was accused of standing by—some say worse.

The charges were never proven. But the stain lingered. So much so that in 2005 the United States denied him a visa under a law that bars entry to foreign officials implicated in religious persecution. For nearly a decade, he was unwelcome in the West.

But then came 2014. And then came 2019.

The Howdy Modi rally in Houston—organized with President Donald Trump—was a celebration of political theater. There were chants, lights, flags, standing ovations—applause louder than any in recent memory.

No one mentioned Gujarat.

No one remembered the ban.

No questions were asked.

Comedian Hasan Minhaj, a child of Indian immigrants and a vocal critic of Modi's policies, tried to attend the rally. He was denied entry.

Ironically, his photo still flashed across the jumbotron—celebrating his success while barring his presence. It was the perfect metaphor for what was unfolding: celebrate the image, suppress the voice.

And still, Modi was never pressed for answers.

Unlike US presidents who must participate in public debates, Modi has never taken part in an open-press interview. He has mastered the art of controlled narrative, appearing strong while silencing dissent.

The documentary *While We Watched* follows Ravish Kumar, one of India's last standing independent journalists. His voice, quiet and resolute, speaks truth in a media landscape that now rewards loyalty over integrity. Watching him is like watching a man shout into a hurricane.

The BBC's documentary on Modi's alleged role in the Gujarat riots was banned within days of its release. Without any debate or without disproving any claims, it was banned.

And just like that, a nation that once prided itself on freedom of expression now muzzles truth like a threat. India now ranks among the lowest in global press freedom.

In 2023, Modi addressed the US Congress and received standing ovations and smiles and polite nods by Biden and Kamala Harris.

No one mentioned the press crackdowns.

No one asked about the bulldozers in Muslim neighborhoods or the vandalized homes of pastors.

No one seemed to remember the visa ban.

Only President Barack Hussain Obama, on his visit to India in 2015, gently but firmly spoke of religious freedom. "Upholding freedom of religion," he said, "is not only the responsibility of government. It is the responsibility of every person."

The Indian media erupted. How dare he? Who was he to comment?

But for the religious minorities in India, he made us feel seen. He understood what it means to stand for those whose voices have been muted. He knew that silence, too, is a decision. And that neutrality in the face of suffering always favors the oppressor.

We all pray, but faith in action means something far more. It means noticing the refugee. The girl turned away at the border. The boy afraid to pray in public. The journalist forced into hiding. The pastor under surveillance. What if instead of building more walls, we sought to build bridges based on understanding? What if we stopped seeing the world as something to defend, and started seeing the people in it—each one of us scared, confused, and searching for a way to be heard?

And then there's the question of freedom. We speak so often about freedom of speech, freedom of expression, but what about the freedom to be safe? To live without fear of hate speech, misinformation, or harassment that erodes one's dignity? Should freedom come at the expense of another's humanity?

What if we dared to uphold a higher standard, one where freedom isn't just about saying what we want, but about ensuring that others can live in peace? Ensuring human dignity means stepping beyond slogans and standing in solidarity with those being oppressed.

I was warned repeatedly not to tell my story. Not for my own safety, but for the safety of those I love and respect. Here I am a proud American. I was born in North Carolina. I carry an American passport. But the heart of our family still pulses with the rhythm of Indian soil. That is the beauty of America; it allows such a space to be. So, I chose to write and share because silence often prolongs the suffering, and I need to let go of this trauma.

The people who stand in solidarity help bring healing, and this I know for sure, suffering is not the end of the story. Jesus reminds us in John 16:33, "In this world, you will have trouble. But take heart! I have overcome the world." These words give us the courage to press on, even when the darkness seems overwhelming.

Perhaps this is my attempt to deal with my own healing, my nostalgia as I let go of the roots planted in my Nana and Nani and Dada and Dadi's gardens, and strengthen my own roots right where I am planted.

The truth is we are all learning to root again, not in the soil of nostalgia but in the truth. The tamarind trees are still with us—in memory, in metaphor. But here beneath the western pines, we are planting again.

The fight for religious freedom, for human dignity, and for compassion is far from over. But we do not fight alone. With every act of kindness, every word of truth, and every moment of courage, we are pushing back against the darkness. We are standing for those who cannot stand for themselves.

So I ask you, even as you read, will you answer the call? Will you stand up even when it's difficult? Will you offer healing where there is hurt?

The world is waiting for your answer. We need new trees, new songs, and renewed courage, bot to return but to remain true to what life needs to speak. So, let us dig deep and root well. Let the gardens grow again. And until

I sing again, I am grateful to be still in the midst of this alpine majesty that feels so alive.

Romans 5:3–5 offers a profound reminder: "we rejoice in our sufferings, because we know that suffering produces perseverance; perseverance, character; and character, hope. And hope does not put us to shame because God's love has been poured into our hearts through the Holy Spirit who has been given to us."

18

The Legacy That Moves On

I've often wondered how exile actually begins. Not the paperwork. Not the plane tickets. Not even the ache of it all. But rather that disorienting unravelling of knowing that the place that raised you forgot about your right to belong.

Christmas at Dada and Dadi's house was a grand celebration. Those childhood memories included people from every walk of life. Diwali, Eid, Holi—we celebrated everything together. The people of Damoh are our own people. We were all one big family with different ways of celebrating. It was all very life-giving, meaningful, uniting. But somewhere in the motherland, there was that unspoken exclusion threaded into every ritual that once felt shared.

That's where stories of exile begin when someone jokes that you are too Christian to be Indian. Someone who used to be a part of every gathering and every celebration, somehow forgets to invite you to the festival. It's not always with fire and fleeing—although that too became part of my family's story. It's a quiet panic of uncertainty that takes over, of safety slipping away. Those headlines that feel more like warnings than stories. When calls drop abruptly midsentence. When prayers start to sound like bargaining.

Even when one becomes both citizen and suspect. Familiar and foreign. Rooted and removed. Joy remained our language that no one could censor.

America has been home for me, but for my loved ones, exile started when they felt like they were breaking open. When we landed in America, the mountains were waiting for us. Friends and loved ones surrounded us with hospitality and care. Lawyers offered to do the paperwork without a hefty fee when we felt too tired to move. Meals were left on our doorstep that helped us regain our strength. People didn't flinch at the mention of persecution. They listened. They encouraged. They supported. In the desert of exile, even a drop of water becomes a spring.

This wasn't Dada and Dadi's garden or the familiar abode of the Himalayas. This was the vast, wild Rockies—steadfast and still. As if to say: You've survived. Now breathe. And that is exactly what we did.

The air was different here. Thinner. Cleaner. Not dense with accusation but fresh and welcoming. There were loved ones who spoke fluent compassion without needing to know the language of our pain.

I don't know if trees can grieve, but sometimes I imagine those palm trees at Maa and Daddy's house and those tamarind trees at Dada and Dadi's house bowed silently after we left. Maybe they too found felt the pain of an exiled soul but rejoice in knowing that in a span of a breath the world becomes home again.

Trauma can try to silence the truth, but truth doesn't forget. It finds its way, and for me, it waited until I could find the words past my tears and grief. It waited for the shaking in my hands to become still. Waited for the stories to rise.

The stories came and when they did, they did not rise like a manifesto but came like flooding memories. Like breath. Like the voices of our loved ones still echoing through those corridors that I may not return to for years—if ever.

But here's the strange thing about grief. It doesn't only linger in sorrow. Sometimes, it curls up quietly in joy. It watches you unwrap laughter after a long silence. It weeps a little when you sing again. It tucks itself into the corner of the room and lets you be.

Christmas 2024 was the first time in years I could feel grief while resting. Not gone. Not forgotten. But resting. Because somehow, miraculously, we had made it. Our loved ones were safe. We were together.

Our entire family—scattered, battle-worn, stitched together by a thousand prayers—was here! Under one roof. Nestled in the embrace of the Rockies, in a home that now held more than our furniture. It held our healing. It held our hallelujahs. It was the most glorious feeling!

My dear husband decked the halls like he was determined to reclaim joy. And reclaim it we did. The snow fell with grace, covering old wounds, softening sharp edges of memory.

The thought of exile certainly doesn't vanish. It lingers. But in the quiet spaces between celebrations, we hold those stories a little lighter. The grace of Christmas reminded us that joy was never tied to geography. We went all out!

There were twinkling lights everywhere, draped along the windows, tangled around railings, tucked behind the nativity scene on the mantle. Lee even hung some from the ceiling fan—because why not? Trauma had made us serious for too long. This was our season to be excessive, to overdo everything that sparkled. There was no such thing as too much light this year. Not after all the darkness we'd come through.

We weren't forgetting our roots; we were adorning them. When the ghosts of all the places we have loved and lost tried to knock on the windows, they remained outside. Inside, there was firelight and forgiveness. There was the laughter of those who survived, who still dare to rejoice. We sang old hymns and carols, not because all was healed but because love made a clearing in the wilderness. The exile could not extinguish the light.

Even the mistletoe we taped above the kitchen entrance felt like a declaration that love lives here.

And we didn't just decorate the house. We decorated our days. Matching pajamas were only the beginning. We cooked too much because we'd been hungry for home, for one another, for the kind of joy that doesn't apologize to taking up space. We drank hot chocolate with way too many marshmallows. We played old-school Christmas music that made us dance like uncles at a wedding reception—awkward, offbeat, and unashamed.

It was cheesy. It was loud. It was glorious.

And underneath all the glitter and silliness, something real was blooming again, something holy. Because this wasn't just about pajamas or peppermint bark. This was about healing. The deep kind. The kind that seeps into your bones only when you stop running. The kind that whispers "it's safe now." You can laugh. You can exhale. You don't have to keep watch tonight. The angels are on duty. And maybe that's why this Christmas felt so sacred, not because of the rituals or the traditions, though those were sweet, but because of what they meant. They were evidence, proof that love had not let go of us. That hope had not failed. That God, in all His mercy, had made a way for joy to return.

We gave thanks to God every day we were together. God does not abandon. We gave thanks for those who chose not to look away. They stood when it would have been easier, safer to turn aside. Our hearts overflow with gratitude when we think of those who fought on our behalf not just in the courts of law but in the unseen courtrooms of conscience.

They did not have to stand with us. But they did, again and again. In the face of lies, of unlawful detention, of rising tides of intimidation they stood. And because they did, we could gather. We could light the candles. We could celebrate Christmas not just as a holiday but as a resurrection.

So we gave thanks not just in prayers but in stories, in song, in the clink of glasses raised not in forgetfulness but in deep, holy remembering. We gave thanks with every child's laughter, every dish passed down the table, every tear wiped away by the hand of someone who stayed.

We gave thanks for the miracle of being together.

As we stepped into 2025 and he snow fell gently outside, we shared with one another this joy, this freedom, this celebration. It was not free. It was fought for, and we will not forget who stood with us in the storm.

How fitting, really, that this joy came at Christmas—the celebration of the birth of our Savior, the Prince of Peace born not in comfort but in chaos, not in a palace but among the poor, not in power but in vulnerability. That has always been the kind of Savior we needed—not the kind who shouts from a distance but the one who steps into the mess. Who comes close. Who enters the exile with us. Jesus, God with us, Emmanuel in every sense.

And this year, more than ever, I understood the miracle of that name. God with us not above us, not beyond us, but with us. In the airports and courtrooms. In the waiting and the wandering. In the ache of leaving and the fragile joy of arriving. He had never left. Even when we were scattered. Even when we thought we couldn't go on. He was there holding, guiding, carrying.

This wasn't just a holiday. It was a holy day, a quiet revolution of the heart because only God could take a family bruised by bureaucracy and exile and wrap us in matching pajamas in a mountain home, singing carols off-key and laughing over burnt cinnamon rolls. Only God could bring beauty from this much brokenness.

And if I'm honest, I think that's what legacy really is—not just what you pass down but what you carry forward.

What you choose to rebuild. What you dare to believe in again.

We are still the grandchildren of Dada and Dadi. The children of Maa and Daddy. Still the carriers of stories from gardens surrounded by imili trees and palm trees and chapel courtyards and how God kept us safe in the midst of those riots. But now, we are also something more. We are witnesses. Testimonies in motion. Evidence that grace has hands and feet and warm blankets and second chances.

We are the ones who know what it is to be lost—and to be found.

We are the ones who carry India in our laughter, who carry faith in our wounds, who carry each other across oceans and altitudes and every kind of border, man-made and otherwise.

And we are still singing. Even now. Especially now because legacy doesn't end in exile. It lives on in every story told around the dinner table. In every candle lit on Christmas Eve. In every act of mercy we choose in a world that prefers revenge. Legacy moves on in the kindness we extend to strangers. In the courage to speak out, to write, to remember. In the prayers we pray for a homeland that may not remember us but that we cannot forget. Legacy is what made us hang up those ridiculous stockings and fill them with tiny gifts and oversized hopes. Legacy is what made us huddle together on that snow-dusted Christmas morning, teary-eyed and pajama-clad, singing "O Come All Ye Faithful" like it was the first time we ever believed it.

Because in some ways, it was.

The Legacy That Moves On

Faith is different after exile. It's less performative. Less perfect. It's more real. More raw. More rooted in survival and resurrection.

It's faith that says, "we're here." Somehow. Against all odds. We're here.

And not just surviving anymore. But living. Rebuilding. Finding rootedness and life again.

There is a special, irreverent kind of joy in cheesy Christmas traditions—the kind that make no theological sense but every emotional one. The matching pajamas, the reindeer antlers, the off-key caroling in four different accents, the dramatic countdown to lighting the star even though the switch is faulty and someone always forgets the extension cord. It's all ridiculous. It's all perfect.

Grief sometimes tries to flood in, but because of prayers and God's protection grief will never take root. It will never have the final word. Love and healing are part of the architecture now.

The final word belongs to joy.

About the Author

Liz Matney is a writer, philanthropist, daughter, sister, wife, and mother of two teenagers. With over two decades of experience working with international humanitarian organizations and advocating for marginalized communities, her work focuses on issues of religious freedom and human rights, particularly in India, where her family has faced threats and systemic harassment. Through her writing, she explores the intersection of identity, belonging, and justice in politically charged environments. She holds a PhD in global leadership and women's studies and has worked extensively in business, non-profit, and educational contexts. After spending a season in India, she and her family are in the process of rediscovering their lives back in the United States. Her diverse background and first-hand experiences uniquely equip her to address complex global issues in a deeply personal way. *Home in Exile* is her debut work, offering a compelling narrative that examines the personal impact of political and social turmoil while engaging with broader conversations on displacement, resilience, and the search for home.

www.ingramcontent.com/pod-product-compliance
Lightning Source LLC
Chambersburg PA
CBHW030220170426
43194CB00007BA/808